DIY
WOOD PALLET
PROJECTS

35 Rustic Modern Upcycling Ideas to *Personalize Your Space*

KARAH BUNDE
of thespacebetweenblog.net

Adamsmedia
Avon, Massachusetts

Published by
Adams Media, a division of F+W Media, Inc.
57 Littlefield Street, Avon, MA 02322. U.S.A.
www.adamsmedia.com

ISBN 10: 1-4405-7447-2
ISBN 13: 978-1-4405-7447-4
eISBN 10: 1-4405-7448-0
eISBN 13: 978-1-4405-7448-1

Printed in the United States of America.

10   9   8   7   6   5   4   3

Many of the designations used by manufacturers and sellers to distinguish their product are claimed as trademarks. Where those designations appear in this book and F+W Media, Inc. was aware of a trademark claim, the designations have been printed with initial capital letters.

Readers are urged to take all appropriate precautions before undertaking any how-to task. Always read and follow instructions and safety warnings for all tools and materials, and call in a professional if the task stretches your abilities too far. Although every effort has been made to provide the best possible information in this book, neither the publisher nor the author are responsible for accidents, injuries, or damage incurred as a result of tasks undertaken by readers. This book is not a substitute for professional services.

Photos by Karah Bunde.
Cover design by Frank Rivera.
Interior spot art © krichanut/Claudiu Badea/123RF.

This book is available at quantity discounts for bulk purchases.
For information, please call 1-800-289-0963.

dedication

to Joel, Marley, and Mico. Our life is my favorite project.

a heartfelt thank-you

to Shane, just know that I know that I hit the jackpot. In the sibling department, that is. I have yet to hit the actual jackpot, but I digress.

to my parents for being supportive and encouraging even when I didn't know I needed it.

to Sue for making me be your person.

and very importantly, to the readers, for without you this journey wouldn't be the same. Your support and encouragement drive me forward. Wait, now you're beginning to sound like my parents.

contents

preface

Hi, my name is Karah and I use items I find along the side of the road to make beautiful things for my home.

Wait, did I just say that out loud?

For over fifteen years, my husband and I have been moving every few years and we're always on the hunt for ways to create a home that we love in a new location. But going the traditional route of shopping for every last item can get pricey. And we all know that some items you find at the thrift shop, even with a coat of a fabulous color of paint and the most fantastic knobs you've ever laid eyes on, aren't ever going to be your style or do anything to help make your space feel like home.

Instead of buying expensive items, or settling for options that just didn't feel quite right, we started making our own things and quickly found that getting creative with pallet wood and designing functional and beautiful items that are a true reflection of our style was the perfect fit for our space and our budget. Before long, I started to chronicle our adventures on my blog, *the space between* (*http://thespacebetweenblog.net*).

With only the limitations of your own imagination, you can surround yourself with things that feel like home even when you're in *the space between*. You know that space—the one between where you've been and where you're going. Wherever that is at this very moment, there's no reason not to make it a space you love and that feels exactly like home.

On the blog you will find us in the midst of a full-house renovation of a 1950s conch-style home in Key West, Florida. The blog journey started in Curaçao (a southern Caribbean island 35 miles east of her more popular sister-island, Aruba), where traditional shopping centers were nonexistent and our most treasured home items were borne out of things I gathered from around the beach, along the road, or out of large construction dumpsters. Now that we're back in the United States, albeit the Caribbean of the United States, and undertaking a home renovation project that will leave no surface untouched, we find ourselves balancing the desire for beautification with the reality of a budget.

My very first pallet project was a simple piece of inspiring word art quickly followed by a pallet wood crate I made as a storage solution in our tiny kitchen in Curaçao. These days, I'm more apt to try to figure out a way to make my own version of any wooden project that I see for sale than I am to actually purchase it. Some people daydream about sunny vacations on the beach, and while I'm living by the beach, I'm the one daydreaming about pallet project possibilities. Yep, I sure do know how to have a good time.

I'm sure you've seen wood pallets around. They are often found near residential or commercial construction sites or on loading docks of your favorite home improvement stores. They are considered trash to those companies, but over the years, through trial and error, I have found ways to transform this "trash" into pieces of furniture and craft or art ideas.

Be it a large or small project, when you let your creativity flow, you have the potential to make an item that will always be one of a kind and unique to your own personal style. And since our main material—wood pallets—doesn't cost anything, we're talking about projects that are all nearly free. And nearly free is a popular price point around here.

In this book, I'm excited to share with you a few of my favorite project ideas along with tips and tricks for finding and working with pallets. Who knows, maybe we'll run into each other at the loading dock of our favorite lumberyard one day.

Until then . . .

enjoy your space today,

Karah ☺

introduction

You might be thinking that wood pallets are an . . . *interesting* starting point for a book of DIY projects. You'll see with the 35 unique ideas in this book that they're a perfect material for a whole range of items—from a clock to an Adirondack-style chair. A few fun facts about the benefits of working with wood pallets are:

▸ you can get them for free
▸ they're amazingly customizable once you take them apart
▸ you only need a few simple woodworking tools to create something great
▸ they have a built-in rustic look
▸ they look great in their natural state—but they hold paint or stain well, too

It has taken almost 15 years—with 5 moves among 2 different countries and furnishing 7 homes on a real-world budget—for me to finally understand my personal style, and that it can't always be found in a store. The ability to create our own things for a fraction of the cost has helped to make every new place feel like home, no matter where we are. My sincere hope is that you find these DIY pallet wood projects inspiring and representative of items you would gladly display around your home and maybe even make you say "Booyah, I made that!" along the way. They are meant to be rustic in nature (it *is* weathered wood, after all) and able to stand up to regular use, with the normal bumps and bruises that come along with everyday life.

These specific designs and instructions can all be tweaked and adjusted to fit your particular space. If you need to, simply add (or subtract) a few inches or feet where necessary to make the pieces fit where you want them to, helping you to create something that will make your space feel just like home to you. The instructions are open to interpretation, too. For example, I may use screws when you want to use nails, or I may use a power saw when you'd feel more comfortable grabbing your handsaw. That's cool; do what works for you.

What you're going to find ahead varies from simple "I've never held a power tool" beginner ideas to projects that might have you saying, "That looks a little challenging, but I'll take it one step at a time and see how it goes." Take it from me: no DIY project is without a little trial and error. I have learned my best lessons after doing something wrong the first (and often a second and third!) time. You will never meet a DIYer who hasn't experienced a project failure; it's just part of the process. If only I had pictures of the very first table my husband and I tried to make! Who knew that terms like *apron* and *stretcher* were actually necessary components to the table-building process? Luckily, it was only for storage in our garage, and through the years, as our knowledge and experience has increased, our projects have continued to improve.

Clearly, not every single project I've ever made has ended up on my blog or in this book. We all have those moments where something just does not turn out quite as planned. Don't be concerned with making the most perfect project ever. I'll warn you now: Perfectly straight pallet slats are hard to come by. But a project's perfection doesn't come in perfectly aligned wood slats. If you create something that you love and are proud of, that's perfection! If a particular project really is a *total* bust, don't let that derail you, either. Grab another pallet and give it another go. Add it to the list of reasons why pallets are so awesome—you don't have to feel bad about trashing a project that started as, well, trash.

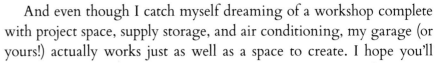

And even though I catch myself dreaming of a workshop complete with project space, supply storage, and air conditioning, my garage (or yours!) actually works just as well as a space to create. I hope you'll

see that even the smallest yard in Key West—where quite often a puppy or two can be found photobombing my most finely arranged shots—is workspace enough to create these projects.

To help everyone get started we're going to talk about some ins and outs of working with wood pallets, including tips and tricks that will help you with each and every project. Thirty-five inspiring project ideas will follow—everything from a statement wall decoration in the form of a Cut-Out Silhouette (see Chapter 2) to a versatile U-Shaped Side Table (see Chapter 6) perfect for a living room or outdoor space. Many of these ideas would also be perfect for a craft night or to make as a gift, like the Miniature Tabletop Tree (see Chapter 4). You'll see how old pallet wood can be sanded and stained to end up looking just like new wood as it did for the seat of the bench (amazing how those pallet slats end up looking almost exactly like the new wood used for the shutters). And then we'll turn around and make a full-length mirror out of brand-new wood we've made to look old and weathered like pallet wood you would have found on the street.

Now just to decide which project to try first.

PART 1
preparation and tools

Here is where you'll find the answers to the most frequently asked questions about pallets and pallet wood. Follow the Q&A format to quickly and easily learn where to find pallets, how to decide which ones are best for your DIY projects, and how to take them apart. Every pallet has telltale signs that you should keep your eyes out for when you're on your search. After reading this, you'll know just what to take home and work into something fabulous. And if you really can't find a wood pallet or don't want to take one apart? No worries! I'll give you other ideas for where to find reclaimed wood to use. You'll also learn about the tools and supplies you'll use to make these projects. Many are regular, everyday items, but you'll also see a few specialty items that could really expand your DIY capabilities as well.

chapter 1
wood pallets 101

I once showed up to a lunch date with a friend and I had a pallet hanging out the back of our Jeep Wrangler. "Where do you find these things?" she asked. That answer and many, many more are in this chapter.

where do I find pallets?

The most failsafe place to find pallets is on the loading dock of a lumberyard, home improvement store, and many other large big-box-style retailers. Pretty much any store that receives large shipments of items, even furniture, will have a supply of pallets. I promise you, once you get into the habit of looking for pallets, you'll start to notice them all around.

Just be sure to ask first before you start grabbing. Some stores have agreements with their shipping companies to return and/or reuse certain pallets. But many are just waiting for the trash collector, and the store will gladly let you take them off their hands. (And if you live in a friendly little community like Key West, Florida, they will even have an employee help you load them in your car.)

Tip!!!

Familiarize yourself with your town's garbage collection days. If you drive around after people have put their trash out for pickup, you might even find something fun to revamp with your pallet wood. Many times, a discarded table or wobbly chair only needs a little TLC to be resurrected into something amazing.

Next time you're at the home improvement store, take a minute to check out the trashcan next to the saw they use to cut wood for customers. You may find some scraps that will be perfect for your next project. Just ask and you might be able to take it home for free.

Keep a special eye out for homes under construction. Don't be shy. Strike up a conversation with ~~strangers~~ the contractors. They will have some great insights for you. Politely ask questions like:

- do you have any pallets I could have right now?
- are you expecting a shipment of materials on pallets anytime soon?
- are you working on any other properties around town that might have pallets available?

After you start asking around, you'll gather a stockpile of pallets in no time.

how should I transport pallets?

Pallets range in size from about 30" square up to 80" long (or more) by about 48" wide. Smaller or midsize pallets will fit right into a sedan's trunk or the back of a small SUV.

If you find a larger pallet and don't have any friends with pickup trucks (which I think is pretty much a necessity in life), you could use bungee cords or rope to secure it to your car's roof rack. Taking a large pallet apart is another way to fit it in your car. (You'll soon learn a few ways to do that.) Just grab your cordless reciprocating saw and cut off the slats you want right where you find the pallet. You might draw a few strange looks from others for carrying around a reciprocating saw in your car, but I'm guessing no one's going to mess with the girl with the saw at the ready.

If that isn't an option for you, a daily truck rental could be your best bet. Many local home improvement stores rent trucks, so that makes for easy, one-stop pallet acquisition.

what do those markings on the pallet mean?

One of the first things to consider before taking a pallet is where it has been and what it has been carrying. You can't trace every pallet back to its maiden voyage, of course, but you *can* judge a lot on its most recent shipment. You can try to get specific information on what was shipped if you're gathering it from a construction site or a store. The loading dock employees see most shipments come and go throughout the day and would be good people to ask. It's a good practice to avoid pallets that have carried chemicals or pesticides or liquid food items, as there may have been spillage onto the pallet along the way.

Pallet wood, like pressure-treated wood you find in the home improvement store, is treated in one way or another, chemically or otherwise. The markings stamped onto the side of the pallet mean something—for example, an "HT" stamp signifies that a pallet has been heat-treated and a "US" stamp indicates it was manufactured in the United States. Keep in mind that these stamps just give you an idea of the history of the pallet, not the complete picture. For example, a heat-treated pallet was kiln-dried when it was manufactured to inhibit bug and insect infestations, but that stamp alone doesn't ensure that, over time, the pallet wasn't subsequently chemically treated by someone other than the manufacturer to extend its lifespan.

the markings on a pallet help you know how it was treated and where it was made

Additional markings make each pallet even more traceable. Refer to regulatory resources online, such as *www.iso.org*, to learn more about the construction of pallets and how they are treated.

These resources can provide you with detailed information about the specifications and regulations regarding the manufacture of wood pallets. This information can further help you decide which pallets to take, based on your comfort level and what you're making. For example, if you're making a wall decoration that no one will touch, you might be okay using a pallet treated with certain chemicals—but you might not feel comfortable making a serving tray from that same pallet. Again, let common sense and your own preferences be your guide.

And if you don't see *any* markings, pick your pallet at your own risk.

how do I know if it's a good pallet to use?

Great question! This information is very important. After all, we are talking about picking up wood pallets from random sources that have shipped unknown products from unknown places and have been touched by an unknown amount of people before you. We have entered the "proceed at your own risk" stage of this process.

Only you know your own personal limits for touching nasty things or encountering bugs, dirt, and grime. While I'm one to hop right into a construction dumpster to snag a wood pallet with the most perfect patina, you may be the one standing horrified on the other side of the road, pointing and gawking at my madness. I have to admit, it wouldn't be the first time.

Some specific things you'll encounter when sourcing pallets are:

- **BUGS/INSECTS/TERMITES**—avoid any pallets with visible evidence of "wildlife." Just in case, it is always a good practice to spray each pallet with an antibacterial spray and scrub it clean after you have it home. (More info on that process in a second.)
- **MOLD**—mold can range in color from shades of green to black and can sometimes even be fuzzy. It is always best to err on the side of caution here, and avoid pallets with visible mold. Buy a mold test kit at a home improvement store if you want to be absolutely sure.
- **EVIDENCE OF LIQUIDS**—any spillage, especially if you don't know the source, should be considered a reason to leave a pallet alone. Avoid pallets that have transported food or liquids—you don't know if the liquid is potentially harmful to work around.
- **UNAPPEALING ODOR**—give it the old smell test and use your common sense. A pallet shouldn't smell like anything, per se. If you sense a strong odor of any kind, it's probably best to leave it be. The smell could be from excessive chemicals or residue from whatever it transported.
- **PAINT**—in my neck of the woods, if a pallet is painted, it signifies that it is one that can be returned by the company for money and is not free for me to take. If you can take a pallet with paint, always make sure it's not lead paint before proceeding with any project.

That may seem like a lot of things to avoid, but here are a few more things you will encounter during your pallet search that *shouldn't* deter you at all:

- **BROKEN SLATS**—many smaller projects can be made using short or broken sections of pallet slats. For example, in projects like the Herringbone Coffee Table (see Chapter 6) and the Pallet Slat–Backed Bookcase (see Chapter 3) where you cut many small pieces anyway, broken slats would work perfectly.

- **RUSTY NAILS**—these will be unavoidable, so don't be afraid to take a pallet with rusty nails. But be sure your tetanus shot is up to date if you are regularly around anything old and rusty.
- **IRREGULAR COLORING**—a unique color combination in your pallet slats can actually help bring a project to life, and, once sanded, many pallet slats take on a different color altogether. The color streaks in the slat I used for the Hook Board with Repurposed Handles (see Chapter 3) add to the dimension of a pretty simple project.
- **KNOTS/NAIL HOLES/SLAT IRREGULARITIES**—what you want to look for specifically in a pallet slat will depend on your project, but knots and nail holes can add a fun detail to a project like the Rustic Wood Clock (see Chapter 2), and the Pallet Slat Tree (see Chapter 4) really came to life with pallet slats in a variety of irregular widths.

Don't ever use pallet wood to make anything on which food will directly sit or that children may find a reason to put in their mouths. Always remember the part about unknown products from unknown places and touched by an unknown amount of people. Words to live by: Pallet projects and food do not go hand in hand.

how do I clean the pallet?

Cleaning your pallet is the first step once you've brought it home. This will get rid of most surface dirt and make the wood project-ready. There are several options for cleaners, and you can basically use whatever you commonly use as an antibacterial cleaner already. If you're looking for an all-natural cleaner, white vinegar is an effective choice. Simply mix 1 part white vinegar and 4 parts water (or more concentrated for dirtier areas), then scrub with a medium-bristle scrub brush.

In addition, bleach has the ability to kill many types of bacteria (you can use the same concentration as the vinegar mixture), and you'll find many antibacterial products on the market that will do the job. Follow the manufacturer's instructions for cleaning wood with these products.

Once you've cleaned the wood, let it air-dry completely before working with it.

how exactly do I get this pallet apart?

Finally! Now we're working. You've scoured your neighborhood, found a pallet that passed all of your safety requirements, brought her home, cleaned her, and now you're ready to take her apart. Following, you'll find step-by-step instructions for four different pallet-dismantling options. I use option 1 the vast majority of the time, but when that gives me more of a challenge than I bargained for, I try one of the other alternatives. There really is no right or wrong way, as long as you keep in mind that safety is always the top priority. When you use power tools, it's sometimes helpful to have a second set of hands available for assistance. Safety glasses are a *must*, and ear protection is recommended to shelter your eardrums from the noise.

Taking a pallet apart can definitely be a workout. But take it slow and steady and remember to focus on safety. If a particular pallet is giving you too much trouble, it probably wasn't meant to be—just move on to the next one.

tools for dismantling a pallet: leather gloves, hammer, pry bar, reciprocating saw, safety goggles, and ear protection (not pictured)

Here are the four main ways I disassemble a pallet:

1. pry off each slat individually from the support boards
2. pry off the support board from the pallet slat
3. cut the nails separating the slats from the support boards
4. cut the pallet slats off the support boards

I know these sound like very similar options, so let's look at each one individually to determine which option is best for you. You might find yourself using one option over another based on the exact construction of the pallet you've found and what you're making. For example, ask yourself:

▸ Are the nails holding the pallet together straight or spiral? Spiral nails are harder to remove—not impossible, just harder.
▸ How many nails were used? If there are more than two or three nails at any given connection, you may want to consider going straight for the reciprocating saw and cutting off the slats to save yourself the trouble of prying off so many nails.
▸ What type of wood do you need for your project? If you want long slats and the added character of the nail holes left in the wood after the nails are removed, prying off each slat is your best option. But if you only need smaller sections of pallet slats, just cutting off the slats would be the quickest way to go.

Before we go any farther, let's look at the parts of a pallet so you know what I'm referring to in the directions.

PALLET SUPPORT BOARDS

PALLET SLATS

parts of a pallet

option 1—pry off each slat individually from the support boards

This is the option I use most frequently. Wedge the curved end of your pry bar in between the pallet slat and the support board, carefully helping it along with your hammer if necessary, and then pry the pallet slat away from the support boards (see image 1). For best results, try to wedge your pry bar in directly under each nail—this will minimize splitting of the wood.

Tip!!!

Just as Rachael Ray would tell you to keep a bowl on the counter for your trash and food scraps while you're cooking, I say keep a bucket nearby to corral rusty nails and broken pieces of pallet slats.

IMAGE 1

After you've managed to pry your pallet slats separate from the pallet support boards, you will need to remove the nails. Use your hammer on the pointed end of each nail to maneuver it out, (see image 2), then pry them from the other side of the pallet slat with the claw end of your hammer by grabbing the head of the nail (see image 3).

IMAGE 2

IMAGE 3

You only need to loosen the nails from the back side enough to get the claw of your hammer under the nail heads on the front side to pry them out. The farther you are able to hammer them through, the easier they will be to remove, but even the littlest gap that enables the claw of your hammer to fit under the head is enough to remove a stubborn nail.

You might encounter ornery nails that don't come right out perfectly. Here are some options in that case:

▸ if the head of the nail bends or breaks off entirely, pull the nail out of the pallet slat with needle-nose pliers: while gripping the nail with the pliers, roll the pliers so the nail wraps around the pliers as it is releasing; this method always seems to be more effective than trying a straight pull
▸ if the nails tend to bend over instead of hammering out, the claw end of the hammer works well to pry them back up straight (see images 4 and 5)
▸ when you're removing a nail that is near the edge of a board, always use the board for leverage; in other words, wedge the claw under the nail head with the head of the hammer resting on the board to give you resistance to pry the nail out (see images 6 and 7)

IMAGE 4

bent nail

IMAGE 5

pull the claw end of a hammer toward you to straighten out any bent nails

IMAGE 6

this way doesn't give you any leverage

IMAGE 7

you will have better luck if you use the board for leverage

option 2—pry off the support board from the pallet

WHAT YOU'LL NEED:
leather gloves,
hammer, pry bar,
safety glasses, and ear
protection

This is very similar to option 1—however, you are now working from the bottom of the slat and prying the support board away from the pallet slat (see image 1). This works great when you're down to the last slat attached to the support.

The support boards on some pallets come with notches in them. Sometimes a project, like the Wine Rack with Stemware Storage (see Chapter 5), is easier to make with these notched support boards. They're like boards with a precut design you can use to your advantage (see image 2).

Tip!!!

Keep all parts of the pallet you're dismantling. They may be usable in one project or another!

IMAGE 1

IMAGE 2

the pallet on the far left does not have notched support boards, while the support boards on the other three pallets each have precut notches

A few whacks of the hammer directly onto the support boards where there are still nails attaching that last slat are sometimes enough to persuade them apart (see image 3).

IMAGE 3

option 3—cut the nails separating the slats from the support boards

If you've got a pallet with a lot of nails attaching each slat, it's going to be time-consuming to use option 1. It's not necessarily difficult to pry them all apart, but it is tiring—so at some point option 3 will become your best choice. This can be a much quicker method, but is also much easier with two people, one to hold the pallet steady while the other works the reciprocating saw.

Carefully place the blade of your reciprocating saw between the wood slat and the support board and cut through the nails (see image 1). You can either use a wood blade that is meant for use on wood with nails in it, or a metal blade.

It really just depends on the look you are going for and the project you are making. This option will leave the rusty nail heads in your pallet slats, but that isn't necessarily a bad thing. If you prefer the nail heads removed, you can use a nail set and a hammer on the cut side of the nails to push the pieces of nail out of the pallet slat.

WHAT YOU'LL NEED: leather gloves, reciprocating saw, safety glasses, ear protection, and an extra set of hands

IMAGE 1

option 4—cut off the pallet slats from the support boards

For any project that only requires short lengths of pallet slat wood, this is by far the quickest and most effective approach. Line up your reciprocating saw blade alongside the pallet support board and cut through each pallet slat (see image 1).

The usable pieces of pallet wood will only be the short sections you've cut off, but this is great for any smaller project and for those pallets that have a lot of extra nails.

WHAT YOU'LL NEED: leather gloves, reciprocating saw, safety glasses, and ear protection

IMAGE 1

what other kinds of wood could I use if I don't want to take a pallet apart?

So, you love the look of the weathered wood but you don't really want to have to go through the trouble of finding and disassembling a pallet?

I hear you!

Have no fear. You have other options for finding reclaimed wood that has a similar look and feel to pallet wood, or to even make brand-new wood look old and weathered. Just like you are reclaiming pallet wood and putting it to use in your own way, you can do the same with all of these other reclaimed wood options. Here are some ideas for other types of reclaimed wood you could use:

the sign is made from a board pulled from our neighbor's garbage pile; the headboard is made out of beadboard found in the crawl space under our house (the opportunities for scrap wood are endless!)

▸ old fence pickets or deck boards
▸ random pieces of wood that your neighbors put out with their garbage
▸ driftwood (one of my favorite wood options, since we've lived near the beach for the last five years)—it may have a more rounded look, since it has been tumbled by the sea, but it still has that same weathered and aged character about it that you can find with pallet wood

Additionally, if you'd rather just buy some wood to create any of these projects, that would work, too. In the lumber aisle, the 1×4 and the 1×6 options are most similar to the size of a pallet slat, and a 2×4 is very similar in size to the pallet support boards. An advantage to store-bought wood is that the boards come in longer lengths, so you expand your options for creating larger projects. But the downside, of course, is the additional cost. Plus, you might want to make the new wood look old. (I've included a chapter in the back of the book that gives you some ideas for techniques to make new wood look old. Check out Chapter 7 for more details.)

There really is no right or wrong way to make any of these projects. Part of the allure of creating pallet wood projects is taking advantage of the opportunity to upcycle something old into something functional and beautiful. But if you don't have pallets at your disposal and you love the look, these projects can easily be made with different kinds of wood.

Tip!!!

The actual size of new wood pieces is not exactly the same as their name. For example, 1×2s are actually ¾" × 1½", 1×6s are ¾" × 5½", and 2×4s are 1½" × 3½". Take these "real" measurements into account as you plan your projects if you're using new wood.

driftwood fish craft on reclaimed wood (for the full tutorial, visit *http://thespacebetweenblog.net/2013/05/16/easy-craft-idea-driftwood-fish/*)

do I have to be a pro at using power tools to do these projects?

Absolutely not! I've included a variety of projects—some of which require very few, if any, power tools—so everyone has a place to start. I don't want you getting frustrated along the way, either, so I've organized each chapter with the projects listed in order of difficulty, with the easiest first. Of course, this is just my opinion. Where I think painting is pretty simple, though sometimes time-consuming, you might disagree. So just use it as a gauge.

The level of difficulty is related more to the number of power tools used and the types of skills needed, like ripping a bevel on a table saw (*ripping a bevel* means cutting a long, straight cut with the blade at an angle down the length of a piece of wood) versus using a cordless drill. Hopefully, once you feel like you've mastered one set of skills, you'll want to graduate to the more complicated projects. And one really cool thing is that many of the techniques you use in one specific project can translate into other projects.

Got the hang of cutting your slats to size and attaching them to support boards to create a rectangle? Awesome! Now you can make any number of art projects ranging from a small craft to sit on your shelf to something 4' tall.

what equipment will I need?

You definitely don't need to be an expert or own a zillion tools to make the projects in this book. But you will need some basic equipment and could greatly benefit from a few specialty items we'll show you here. You most likely own at least some of these items already. For any item you don't have, here are a few options to consider:

- buy items new, says Captain Obvious
- rent tools from a local store
- look online on sites such as craigslist or eBay for inexpensive, used tools
- purchase used items from estate sales, thrift shops, or a Habitat for Humanity ReStore (this option is probably best for hand tools, since these sales are generally final and warranties are not offered on power tools)
- borrow them from a friend or neighbor

Let's start with the most basic of tools.

a pencil

Let's talk about the pencil for a second. You should always have one on hand when you're working on projects. Whether it's to jot down measurements, make your marks for cutting, or just to start a grocery list when you remember you need milk in the middle of a project, a pencil is just a project necessity.

everything else

I'll share a few tips and tricks specific to the project tutorials along the way, but I encourage you to practice, practice, practice with your tools and equipment. Spend an afternoon just making practice cuts to familiarize yourself with your saws. Set the blade to different angles and get a feel for how it works. These projects are just the beginning of what you can create with your tools.

With that said, here are a few tools, supplies, and concepts that we use in the book that will be helpful as you create these projects.

Tip!!!

This book is by no means intended to be a tool instructional manual. There are a number of resources available online as well as books and video tutorials that are specific to tool instruction. Start with the projects that require the use of tools that you are comfortable with, but don't shy away from trying new things. Always read a new tool's instructional guide and safety details before getting started and practice all of the appropriate precautions while using the tool.

this variety of basic tools and supplies will help you create many of the projects in this book

Some of my favorite hand tools include:

- **CARPENTER'S SQUARE (ALSO KNOWN AS A FRAMING SQUARE OR STEEL SQUARE)**—this 24" × 16" L-shaped tool is great for verifying 90° angles on larger pieces of furniture and marking long, straight lines
- **CLAMPS**—a good pair of clamps will give glue the extra support it needs to bind properly while it is curing; clamps are also helpful to hold items in place while you're making small cuts
- **EAR PLUGS**—to delay that inevitable hearing loss
- **HAMMER**—kind of self-explanatory, no?
- **HANDSAW**—a good-quality handsaw works great for short, straight cuts; look for one with a blade made of high-quality steel and thick enough to endure hardwood cuts
- **LEATHER GLOVES**—leather gloves really protect your hands against splinters and callousing; a sturdy pair of leather gloves is a smart investment, as they provide more protection than a basic cotton pair
- **LEVEL**—technically called a plumber's level, the small size of this tool is handy for small to midsize projects
- **NAILS AND SCREWS**—one of these options is used in pretty much every project in this book; you can decide which works best for you, but screws provide more stability for furniture pieces
- **NAIL SET**—use this with a hammer to set your nails deep into the wood; then you can plug the tiny hole with wood filler if desired to hide any evidence of the nails
- **NEEDLE-NOSE PLIERS**—the small size and pointed end of these pliers make it a great tool for anything from coiling wire to removing nails
- **PRY BAR**—this tool is invaluable when it comes to taking pallets apart
- **SAFETY GLASSES**—always a smart idea when working with wood and using any power tool
- **SANDPAPER**—keep a variety of grits of sandpaper handy to help with anything from removing splintery wood to softening your project; the higher the grit number of the sandpaper, the finer the finish you will achieve
- **SAWHORSES**—not pictured here, but used frequently throughout the book, a sturdy set of sawhorses can be used as a surface to support your project materials or even as a base for your miter saw; plus, sometimes it's just nice to not have to crouch down to the ground to work

- ▸ **SPEED SQUARE**—this small triangular-shaped square is great for a quick double check of square and also for marking 45° angle cuts
- ▸ **STRAIGHTEDGE**—technically more of a term than a tool, but keeping a long, straight piece of scrap wood, a yard stick, or maybe a 4' level nearby will help in making long, straight marks
- ▸ **TAPE MEASURE**—you know, to measure
- ▸ **WOOD GLUE**—glue, when combined with screws, will provide the strongest hold at the connections of the items you build over time, but if you ever want to be able to take something apart, you might want to choose to skip the glue

can you tell me more about the saws I'll be using?

Let's talk about cutting and saws for a minute. You will see the tool "saw" referenced in many a tutorial. Unless I think there is really only *one* saw option for specific cuts, I'll let you decide which saw you want to use. Most frequently I use my electric **miter saw** for cuts that just shorten a board's length. You might not have one, so I don't want you to think that is a specific requirement. A hand miter saw will often work—or even a jigsaw. If you think woodworking is going to become a prominent part of your future, an investment in an electric miter saw will end up saving you a bunch of time, and often headaches, down the road.

a miter saw, whether electric or not, will make cutting mitered corners quick and easy

what power tools might I need?

These projects really can't come to life without:

palm sander and cordless drill

It still amazes me what a difference there is in the appearance of sanded pallet slats versus unsanded pallet slats. Using a **palm sander** to create a smooth surface on the wood (be sure to run the sander in the same direction as the wood grain) and running it over the edges to create a softer, rounder corner can add just the right detail to take your project from literally trash to treasure.

And where would we be if we still needed to screw in everything by hand with either flat-head or Phillips screwdrivers? Miserable, that's where we'd be. Insert a ⅛" drill bit into your **cordless drill** and you can quickly drill pilot holes into your pallet slats to prevent the wood from splitting when you screw them together. And with the appropriate screwdriver bit (depending on the screws you are using), the cordless drill can make quick work of fastening even a long screw into hard wood. For these reasons, I reference using a cordless drill in these projects. But, hey, this is a judgment-free zone, so grab those hand screwdrivers if you'd prefer.

A couple of upgraded tool options that really help move the building process along:

a nail gun and impact driver are two tools that could really save you time

While a hammer and nail work great for many projects, this battery-operated **nail gun** is a fun tool to have around to make quick work of many projects that are nailed together. And while a standard cordless drill will often do the trick, the added benefits of rotational and downward force provided with an **impact driver** can work wonders with even the hardest wood and longest screws.

If I were to make one recommendation of a small tool that could change the way you DIY:

Especially when you're making items like furniture (see Chapter 6), the sturdiness of the piece will depend on the strength at the joints, where two different pieces of wood are joined. Using the **pocket hole jig** is an easy and effective way of strengthening a simple butt joint by drilling a pocket hole with the

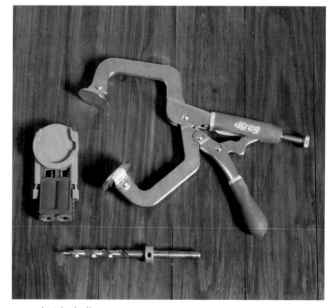

a pocket hole jig

drill bit provided with the jig at an angle where you will then countersink your screws to connect the joint securely. Many of the projects in this book, including a few of the larger items such as the Large Dog Bed (see Chapter 6), Planter Box with Mitered Corners (see Chapter 5), and the Wine Rack with Stemware Storage (see Chapter 5), can be made without drilling pocket holes, but this tool is one to consider if you're looking to expand your arsenal.

what does the sandpaper grit number really tell me?

Now, I may think that 100-grit sandpaper is the best invention ever ~~behind wine and cheese, of course~~. So when I refer to medium-grit sandpaper, that is probably what I'm using. Some determining factors for what grit you choose to use will be how rough the wood is to start with and how smooth of a finish you want. The higher the grit number, the finer the grit and the smoother the finish you will achieve. For example, I stripped and sanded the wood slat walls in our house, starting with 100 grit, then using 150 grit, and finishing up with 220 grit to get an incredibly smooth finish. Since part of the charm of pallet wood is its rustic nature, I don't see the need to get the wood super smooth, but your opinion may differ. And you may find some pallet slats that start out incredibly rough with a lot of splintery edges. In those cases, you may even want to start with a more course grit, like a 60-grit sandpaper, and work toward a finer grit from there. A 150-grit sandpaper is the finest grit I used for projects in this book, but the higher the number you choose, the smoother your project will become.

I use an electric palm sander as well. I say, why use my own elbow grease when I can employ a machine to do the work for me? But that doesn't mean that hand sanding can't get the job done. Just consider it your upper-body workout for the day. You'll notice that the palm sander is always listed in the tools section as optional—hand sanding works just fine, too.

who's ready to create something awesome?

You're very, very close to Part 2 of this book, where we dive headfirst into making some pretty cool things out of pallets. Each project defines the supplies and tools you will need as well as a cost investment (if any). Since the main material in all of the projects is pallet wood or a similar equivalent, any cost is pretty minimal. And I always advocate using what you have on hand. So if the tutorial specifies

Tip!!!

It's always a smart idea to wear a mask or a respirator whenever you're cleaning and sanding any kind of wood, especially reclaimed wood.

1×2 wood pieces or ¾" plywood and you have something similar on hand left over from another project, use that instead and adjust your measurements accordingly. Part of the fun of working with reclaimed items is the ability to make it custom and one of a kind. Scrounge around your shed or garage and try to use up as many as possible of those little wood scraps and old hardware and hinges that seem to accumulate over time. And keep an eye out for funky hardware and knobs on furniture at thrift shops—you never know when something might just be the perfect fit for a future project.

With each project tutorial I've included an "investment" section. This is my best guess of the amount of time and resources you will need to invest in each project. Keep in mind that this is just me guessing how long it will take you to complete something, but since we probably haven't even met, who am I to gauge that? This investment guide is purely meant to give you a bit of an expectation so you can plan accordingly, whether you're looking for something to whip up easily on a late weekend night or something more intricate.

The bottom line is just to work at your own pace and in your own style. I am often in the middle of a plethora of different projects at once. I'm not necessarily advocating that approach, especially if you're one to thrive on order and organization, but if one particular project is giving you grief, switch it up. Tackle a different piece and come back to show that trouble project who's boss another day.

One last thought before you go: Keep in mind, there are many fun ways to personalize and embellish your own projects. Some of the projects include optional steps for finishing touches, but don't stop there. Use your favorite paint colors, stencil on meaningful numbers, or change the shape of a certain project. Make each project representative of your own personal taste and style. Refer to Chapter 7 to see examples of some of my favorite ideas and use them to get your creative juices flowing.

Use this book and these project ideas as a starting point; you can also find many more project ideas on my blog (*http://thespacebetweenblog.net*). Take the inspiration and let your imagination run wild. I can't wait to see what you create!

project tutorials

the beginning of every project

Ahead you are going to find specific tutorials for a number of eclectic, unique, and rustic project ideas made out of pallet slats and reclaimed wood alternatives. Since the base of each project is wood, the first few steps of each tutorial are the same so I've included them all here instead of repeating them with every project. All of the details for the steps itemized here can be found in Chapter 1.

1. select your wood of choice
2. if you're using pallet wood, remove the slats from the pallet support boards
3. remove the nails from the slats
4. clean your wood and let it dry completely

Now you are ready to create something one of a kind. Here are a few more things to keep in mind as you move ahead:

▸ Many of the pallet slats that I've gathered measure a thickness of ⅝" but are imperfect cuts. They may be slightly thicker at one end or even slightly wider in various sections of the individual pallet slat. The length of the nails and screws used for each project in this book is what worked for the specific wood that I used. Be sure to measure your pallet slats (or fence pickets or reclaimed wood) before you start any individual project to ensure you use the correct length of fastener for your specific wood.

▸ The imperfections in each board may also affect your cuts. Embrace the imperfections and don't let them hinder your progress. If a mitered corner doesn't line up perfectly or one slat sticks out a little farther than another, I like to call that "character." Let's just say my house is filled with character.

Now, on to the projects!

chapter 2
getting crafty

In this chapter you will find ideas for projects that not only can be great additions to your own home, but could make great gift ideas, too. We start with a simple yet quirky idea for a clock and proceed to a variety of picture frame options—including one that is even the right size to cover up a full-size electric panel. Sometimes it's fun just to take some time to make something crafty, even if it doesn't serve a specific purpose. Remember to check out Chapter 7 for ways to finish off these projects. Although I have left them mostly plain, you could choose to embellish your own projects with paint or rope or maybe even lettering so they will be the perfect fit for your own space.

rustic wood clock

It seems like everywhere I turn these days when I'm in any store that offers home decor items I see a large, round-faced, wood slat–looking clock for sale. So I say to myself what every DIYer says to themselves when they see an item they like in a store: "I could totally make that." So I did! This specific tutorial is for a 19"-diameter circle clock. You could adjust the size or even get creative with your own clock shape. The clock will function properly as long as you install the clock kit directly in the center of whatever shape you choose—oval, maybe? To hang the clock, I ended up just nailing a small nail into our wall and using the top 1×2 piece that connects the slats together to hang it, but you could also add a picture hanger.

And, just to show how projects tend to evolve, after I had the project complete and photos done I thought a little rope could be the perfect finishing touch around the edges. It's definitely not a requirement, but it's a fun addition to finish off the edge of this project.

supplies needed to make a pallet slat clock

INVESTMENT: about an hour of construction, depending on how quick of a painter you are, and the cost of a clock kit

SUPPLIES

‣ 5 wood slats or partial slats

‣ 1 nail

‣ string, at least 4" longer than the desired radius of your clock

‣ 2 (1×2) wood pieces, cut 15" long

‣ wood glue

‣ medium-grit sandpaper

‣ clock kit

‣ paint and craft paintbrush

‣ rope (optional)

‣ painter's tape (optional)

‣ 6–8 (1¼") nails

TOOLS

‣ hammer

‣ tape measure

‣ jigsaw

‣ clamps or a heavy object (optional)

‣ palm sander (optional)

‣ drill and bit based on the size of your clock kit

‣ adjustable wrench (optional)

‣ serrated knife (optional)

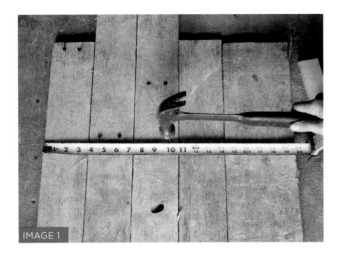

IMAGE 1

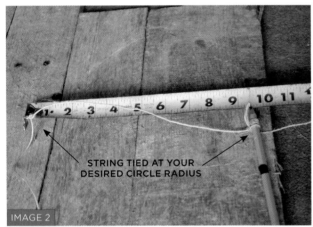

STRING TIED AT YOUR
DESIRED CIRCLE RADIUS

IMAGE 2

IMAGE 3

1 Lay your slats side by side vertically and hammer the nail into the center point, only about ½" deep (see image 1).

2 Tie string around the nail and measure to extend it 9½" (or to your desired length). Tie the other end of the string around your pencil (see image 2).

3 Pulling the string taught, draw a circle around the nail (see image 3).

4 Remove the nail.

5 Cut each slat on your mark with a jigsaw (see image 4).

6 Lay the 1×2s horizontally on their flat side. When deciding where to lay the 1×2s, be sure to avoid the exact center point and a couple inches around it to leave room for the clock kit, and keep in mind where any holes are in your pallet slats. Avoid

IMAGE 4

it's handy to use a set of sawhorses while jigsawing, but any ledge will work

those spots as well so the 1×2s aren't seen from the front of the clock. Run beads of wood glue along each 1×2 (see image 5).

7 Lay your cut pallet slats in the shape of your circle on top of the glue and 1×2s (see image 5).

8 Use clamps or place a heavy object on top for additional pressure if desired. Let the glue dry overnight.

9 Sand the entire circle with a palm sander and medium-grit sandpaper.

10 Drill through the center of your circle and install the clock kit as directed on the packaging (see image 6).

11 Add numbers (see image 7). Even though I started by trying to use a paint pen, I found that simply sketching the Roman numerals first with a pencil to ensure proper alignment and then painting them on with a small craft paintbrush worked best for me.

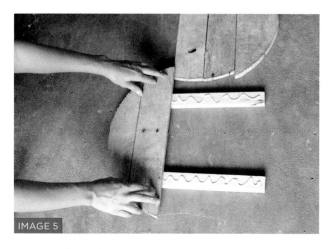

IMAGE 5

IMAGE 6

although my clock kit didn't indicate it, I found an adjustable wrench to be helpful with the assembly

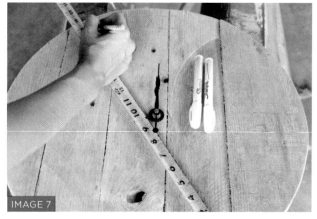

IMAGE 7

use a tape measure or a straightedge to line up the opposing numbers; i.e., 2 and 8, 5 and 11, etc.

variation—rope-edged clock

ADD ROPE DETAIL IF DESIRED: Measure the diameter of your clock and then measure that same distance on your length of rope. Wrap painter's tape around the rope at that point, then use a serrated knife to cut the rope through the painter's tape (this will prevent the rope from fraying). Hammer 1¼″ nails through the rope into the edge of the clock (see image 8). Nails with a wide head on them will hold the rope in place well.

IMAGE 8

Tip!!!

Instead of remeasuring to find the center point to install your clock kit, use the little hole left from the nail you used to tie your string as your center point. Unless you really messed up your circle, then don't do that and just measure.

picture frames—3 ways

Who doesn't love to display photographs, memorabilia, and other sentimental items in neat frames around the house? If you're someone who likes the look of rustic wood, using it as a backdrop for your most prized possessions is a no-brainer. Make two or three of one style of picture frame to create a uniform-looking grouping of photos or artwork, or make one of each style to display together for a more eclectic look that is unified by the use of the pallet wood.

pallet slat picture holder

The first option was inspired by a gift I received from my in-laws. The simple wood backdrop provides the perfect surface for a rustic photo display. The measurements in the tutorial work well for 5" × 7" photos. A good guide to keep in mind as you create your own is to make the frame about 8" taller and 4" wider than your photo. But I also love the look of a really wide mat board with a smaller, usually square, photo in the center. For that look, you could make your wood slats overhang your photo by up to 10" on each side, depending on the size of your photo.

1 Use your tape measure to measure your photo and use a miter or handsaw to cut your pallet slats to a length about 8″ longer than the height of your photo; mine are cut 13″. You will probably need 3–5 slat pieces cut this length depending on the size of your photo.

2 Lay your cut slats side by side with the slats running vertically and use your tape measure to measure the width of them all together.

3 Use a miter or handsaw to cut the 1×2s to this measurement (see image 1).

4 Use your palm sander and medium-grit sandpaper to sand each wood piece individually. Running the sandpaper along the corners of the wood pieces will give them a rounded edge.

5 Run a bead of wood glue on the flat side of each 1×2 and use your hammer or nail gun to attach the 1×2s to the pallet slats with the nails. Each 1×2 runs horizontally across each slat and is lined up based on your personal preference. The 1×2s shown in this photo are inset ¾″ from the top and bottom, but could also be lined right up with the ends depending on which look you like better (see image 2).

6 Use your photo as a guide to determine where to hot glue each of your small clips onto the wood slats. Put them at the top corners of the photo you will be displaying to help prevent the photo from curling over time (see image 3).

7 Use your glue gun to hot glue the clips in place and let the glue dry.

8 Clip on your photo and enjoy!

IMAGE 1

all of the wood components before sanding

IMAGE 2

IMAGE 3

barnwood picture frame

INVESTMENT: this frame takes less than an hour to make and doesn't cost a thing if you use pallet slats; you could also purchase 1×4s and 1×2s to make this same design with new wood

SUPPLIES

- 3 pallet slats at least 33" long
- medium-grit sandpaper (optional)
- wood glue
- 1¼" nails
- 2" nails

TOOLS

- tape measure
- miter saw
- table saw
- palm sander (optional)
- hammer or nail gun

This frame design has an inset on the back side, so you could insert a piece of cut glass or plexiglass for a traditional framed-picture look. But this frame also works really well to showcase your three-dimensional art. Maybe attach a set of eclectic old keys to a mat board or glue shells in a row from your last summer vacation. This tutorial is for a frame that will display a full 8" × 10" photo. But be sure to double-check your measurements, as they will vary depending on the thickness of the pallet slats you are using.

1 Use your miter saw to cut 2 pallet slats with mitered corners at 45° on the flat side. You want to end up with 2 pieces that are 8″ long on the short side and 2 pieces that are 10″ long on the short side.

2 Use your table saw to rip 1 pallet slat into 2 strips 1¼″ wide. (Anytime you cut along the length of a board, as opposed to along its width, it is called a rip cut.)

3 Use your miter saw to miter each corner of the 1¼″-wide strips at 45° on the edge side, so you have 2 pieces measuring 13¾″ long on the short side and 2 pieces measuring 15¾″ long on the short side (see images 1 and 2).

IMAGE 1

mitering a 45° angle on the edge side

Tip!!!

Instead of measuring the outer frame pieces using a tape measure, you can use the already mitered cuts of the inner frame pieces as a guide. The short side of the outer frame piece should measure the same length as the long side of the inner frame piece.

measuring the outer piece of the frame using the inner piece that has already been cut to size

IMAGE 2

finished wood cuts, from left to right: mitered on the edge side, 15¾″ long on the short side; mitered on the flat side, 10″ long on the short side; mitered on the flat side, 8″ long on the short side; mitered on the edge side, 13¾″ long on the short side

project continued on next page

IMAGE 3

4 Use your palm sander and medium-grit sand-paper to sand each individual piece if desired. The really rustic look of the unsanded wood is nice too, so it's your choice.

5 Attach the pieces mitered on the flat side first. Run a bead of wood glue along the mitered corners and nail in a 1¼" nail close to the outside tip of the corner, and then a 2" nail about 1" away from the first nail, per corner (see image 3).

6 Attach the pieces mitered on the edge side around the outside of the pieces you just at-tached. Run a bead of glue and nail them together with 1¼" nails into the outer edge of the pieces already attached. Be sure to put a few nails right in each corner to ensure a tight fit and then add a few more along each piece (see images 4 and 5).

IMAGE 4

the outer frame can overlap the inner frame by about ¼" both in the front and the back creating a lip to insert glass if desired

IMAGE 5

variation—simple jewelry organizer

This project is one part picture frame, one part advent calendar, and one part hook board. Confused yet? It's actually a combination of a few projects in other parts of this book melded into one. It's the perfect place to corral all of that costume jewelry and dangly earrings that are stashed away in a jewelry box somewhere. I think this would be so great hung on a wall in a master closet—it's like art for the closet walls, but it's functional storage space as well. Two birds, one project stone.

INVESTMENT: a few hours and some organizational fun for stylish storage solution geeks like me

TOOLS

‣ see individual projects listed in instructions

SUPPLIES

‣ see individual projects listed in instructions

1   Make the Barnwood Picture Frame from Chapter 2 to serve as a frame and wire holder.

2   Add the eye hooks and wire from the Rustic Advent Calendar tutorial in Chapter 4 to the back side of the frame. Attach 1 strand of wire near the top of the frame to hang only long pieces, or use multiple strands if you have more shorter things to hang.

3   Finish off the area following the Hook Board with Repurposed Handles tutorial from Chapter 3. These hooks will add character and can hold anything from long necklaces to heavier pieces like scarves or belts.

Tip!!!

You could also add knobs and hardware right to the frame instead of using a separate hook board—or you could use both, depending on how big your jewelry ~~problem~~ collection is

the perfect Instagram picture frame

INVESTMENT: a few hours of time to create and the cost to get a handful of your Instagram pictures printed

SUPPLIES

- 20 pallet slat pieces measuring 3½" × 7"
- 8 pallet slat pieces measuring 3½" × 3½"
- medium-grit sandpaper
- 1⅛" screws
- 2 pallet slats 1¾" wide × 21" on the short side with the flat side mitered at a 45° angle
- 2 pallet slats 1¾" wide × 35" on the short side with the flat side mitered at a 45° angle
- 2 pallet slats 1½" wide × 24⅝" on the short side with the edge side mitered at a 45° angle
- 2 pallet slats 1½" wide × 38¾" on the short side with the edge side mitered at a 45° angle
- 1½" nails

TOOLS

- tape measure
- miter or handsaw
- table saw (to rip the frame pieces; if you'd like to keep them full width, you don't need a table saw)
- palm sander (optional)
- pocket hole jig
- clamp
- cordless drill
- hammer or nail gun

This project is the perfect example of an idea developing over time. One of the first things we had to do when we bought our house in Key West was to update the electrical wiring, including installing a brand-new circuit breaker box *right* in the middle of our main living area. We tried to think of ideas to hide her, but she's an awkward size measuring 39" tall and 15½" wide and she's nestled between a corner and a window. The idea for the Geometric Wall Art actually came to me when I was making the Welcome Mat in Chapter 5. But what started as just a fun arrangement of wood quickly turned into a fun arrangement of wood with openings to display photos! (Anyone else infatuated with Instagram? I'm @thespacebetweenblog if you're on Instagram, too.) The outer frame of this piece adds a cool look, plus it means that the frame will hang flush with the wall on all four sides even after you attach pictures from the back side.

1 With a miter or handsaw, cut all of the wood pieces to size. You may want to keep the frame pieces a little long just to give yourself leeway to trim them to the exact size once the design is assembled.

2 Lay out your design. For this specific design, take 4 of the 3½" × 7" pieces and create a square with a 3½" × 3½" opening in the middle and measuring 10½" on each outside edge. Each 3½" × 7" piece will end up as one side of two different squares. The 3½" × 3½" pieces will fill in around the edges to create a rectangular design (see image 1).

3 Keeping your design in order, flip each piece over so the front of your design is facing down and mark where to drill pocket holes (see image 2). I also found it helpful to scribble a numbered guide (with arrows indicating if the piece was running horizontally or vertically) starting from the top left corner and numbering across each "row," on the back of each piece. You will need 2 pocket holes in one end of each 3½" × 7" piece to connect each of your squares, and you will want enough pocket holes to connect each square to the other squares to give stability to the finished product.

Tip!!!

Take a picture of your design for quick reference in case you get them mixed up while flipping them over or drilling the pocket holes. You could also number each piece (as shown in image 2) and use arrows to indicate which direction they should lay.

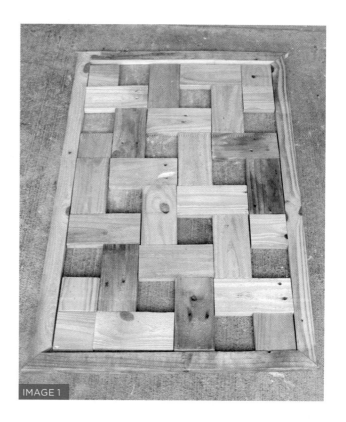
IMAGE 1

IMAGE 2

project continued on next page

IMAGE 3

IMAGE 4

be sure you mark holes to attach your frame pieces that aren't in the same spots where you already have screws connecting the design pieces together

4 Use your palm sander and medium-grit sand-paper to sand each piece. It is easier to sand each piece individually before everything is attached.

5 With your design still lying face-down so you can see your marks, take 3 or 4 pieces at a time and drill the pocket holes with your pocket hole jig. Follow the instructions on your pocket hole jig to clamp each piece of wood in place to drill your pocket holes. Then use your cordless drill to attach each piece together with 1⅛" screws (see image 3). Repeat the pocket-hole-drilling process with groups of 3 or 4 pieces of wood at a time, always connect-ing the new set of 3 or 4 pieces to the previous set. As the frame takes shape, make any adjustment to where you will drill pocket holes based on how the pieces are connecting together. This process is more time-consuming than it is difficult. All in all, I ended up using 66 screws to connect all the pieces.

6 Lay down your completely attached design with the front facing up now, and let's attach the frame. Line up the wood pieces mitered on the flat side around your design and mark on the back of the frame where to drill pocket holes (see image 4).

7 Drill pocket holes with your pocket hole jig in the frame pieces.

8 With your pocket holes drilled, but not yet screwed in, attach the mitered corners of the frame pieces together with 1 or 2 (1½") nails per corner. (This will help them stay lined up while you attach them all around through the pocket holes.) The pocket holes will be slightly visible from the side view (see images 5 and 6).

attaching the mitered frame

the pocket holes are visible now but will be covered in the next step

9 To hide those pocket hole marks, you can add a second edge around the frame. Line up each piece that is mitered on the edge side around the frame piece you just attached and attach the outer frame pieces with nails. I used the same 1½" size because I had them, but you could also use a 1" nail here if desired.

a few fun memories to display, like 1) our first day at the dog park here in Key West when both of the girls just hung by my legs watching all of the other dogs play, 2) that time the hardware store made me put Marley in a cart, and 3) the day Mico spontaneously stuck her head out the sunroof and let her jowls flap in the wind

variation—geometric wall art

Unique wall art is something that can make quite a statement in a home. At this size, this piece can also cover up a standard circuit breaker box (ours is tragically right in the middle of our main living areas). If you don't want to leave the openings bare, the design of this piece is perfect to showcase an interesting fabric. Since you don't need a lot of fabric, you could splurge on a small piece of an expensive textured fabric, or just look at your fabric store's remnant bin for a frugal find. Also, with the design of the raised frame it leaves enough of a gap between the art piece and your wall to add rope lighting! (That idea comes to you courtesy of my husband.) Run some rope lighting hidden back in there to illuminate the fabric, or empty openings, from behind and give off a little glow. You end up with a unique art piece to display.

1 You'll make the frame exactly the same as in the previous tutorial for The Perfect Instagram Picture Frame. This idea just shows how you can mix things up to make the same frame look very different.

2 Painter's tape works great to attach fabric to the back and keep it easy to change out so you can always display your current pattern or color fascination.

3 This piece is finished off with a very pale shade of aqua paint—just a combination of a couple of sample paint pots I already had on hand. But the rustic wood would be a nice look, too.

INVESTMENT: a few hours and the price of a remnant piece of fabric … and maybe some rope lighting

SUPPLIES

‣ see The Perfect Instagram Picture Frame tutorial

TOOLS

‣ see The Perfect Instagram Picture Frame tutorial

cut-out silhouette

INVESTMENT: only an hour or so of your time

SUPPLIES

‣ inspiration picture
‣ 4 pallet slats
‣ medium-grit sandpaper (optional)
‣ pallet support boards (to use as the backing boards that attach the entire silhouette piece together—if you don't have any available, you can use 1×4s instead)
‣ wood glue
‣ 1¼" nails

TOOLS

‣ sawhorse
‣ jigsaw
‣ palm sander (optional)
‣ tape measure
‣ miter or handsaw
‣ hammer or nail gun
‣ clamps or a heavy object

Silhouette art is one of the simplest ways to bring design into your space without needing to be a real artist. Or even a pretend artist. Trust me, I have the artistic abilities of a wasp (They can't be in the least bit artistic, right?!) and even I have successfully created over half a dozen different silhouette art pieces. My first inspiration for a silhouette project was our beloved pups, and they were simply painted on canvas. I used my own digital photographs enlarged and printed on our home printer and traced onto the canvases.

If you don't have a personal photograph that you'd like to use for this wood pallet project, a quick Google image search is a great way to find an image you like. Just remember that this type of art is only going to have an outline, or silhouette, so images that require a lot of detail inside a shape to give it structure won't translate well.

This project would also make a great gift—a monogram or the year in silhouette art could be wedding present perfection. For my pallet project, I thought a whale image would be fun to bring in more of that rustic nautical feel I am trying to create in our home. A sea turtle would also look neat. Or, I grew up on a farm, so what about a

cow image if that fits with your motif? Or, a buck's head image for a woodsy feel? The options truly are endless. And because I'm sucker for a simple art project, we're going to delve into two different ways to make silhouette art with pallet wood. (You can find the second silhouette option in Chapter 4; it has a holiday flare to it.)

for the canvas silhouette full tutorial, go to *http://thespacebetweenblog.net/2012/02/09/diy-canvas-silhouettes*

1   Select your image and align your pallet slats side by side to create a surface big enough to transfer your image. Don't cut the slats yet; leave them longer/wider than you need.

2   Trace (or draw, if you are the artsy type) your image onto the pallet wood (see image 1).

IMAGE 1

Tip!!!

A Google image search or even basic clip art are good places to find images that would work well to make into silhouette art. If you can't blow up your image to be the right scale for your project, divide your printed image into equal-size sections and then mark in pencil the same number of equal-size sections on your pallet slats; then free-hand draw one section at a time on a larger scale onto your pallet canvas.

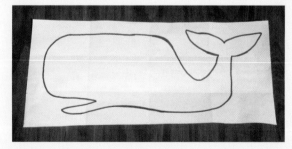

fold the paper into equal sections to make a grid to easily enlarge your image

3   With the image traced, but not yet cut, double-check your drawn image to make sure that when you cut it out you will be able to attach all of your slats together from the back without interfering with your silhouette cutout. For example, if any section of your image as drawn will be hard to cut out and maintain the integrity of the image, you may want to make minor adjustments to your drawing to accommodate for that.

4   Supported by a sawhorse (or anything where you have space below your slat for your jigsaw blade), cut out along the traced line with a jigsaw, cutting each slat individually. When cutting, remember you are keeping the outside of the image. Err to the inside of your drawing if possible. You can always cut more if need be, but you can't ever get back what you've already cut. If a particular cut goes totally awry, just find a replacement pallet slat and start that piece over. There's no real pressure here at all. It's wood you've salvaged anyway, so take as many tries as you need to get it right (see image 2).

IMAGE 2

project continued on next page

5 Use your palm sander and medium-grit sandpaper to sand all cut edges (see image 3). Realign cut pieces to ensure the image lines match up from one slat to the next.

6 Use your tape measure to measure the height of your art piece at each end (or skip the tape measure and just line up the boards you're using for the backing boards) and mark where to cut (see image 4). Also measure any inner areas of your silhouette that will need additional boards attaching them from the back.

7 Use a miter or handsaw to cut your backing board pieces to length.

8 Lay each backing board vertically on its flat side and run a bead of glue on top of it. Place each cut pallet slat horizontally in place with the ends lined up with the edge of the backing board (see image 5). Repeat this step with the other backing board, placing it at the other end of the pallets slats.

9 To strengthen the connection of the glued pieces, use 1¼" nails and a hammer or nail gun

IMAGE 3

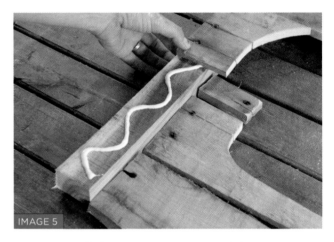

IMAGE 5

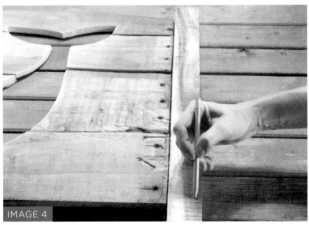

IMAGE 4

IMAGE 6

to nail each individual slat into the backing board. Use 2–4 nails in each end of each slat.

10 For the middle pieces, run a bead of glue on the flat side of your support piece then line up your cut pieces on top (see image 6).

IMAGE 7

the piece that you can barely see under the cement block is getting glued to the art piece; the shim piece you see sticking out into the silhouette is only there to hold the narrow, cut section of the design in place so it is lined up properly with the pallet slat above it; once the glue has dried, that extra shim will not be part of the finished project

11 To avoid nail holes in the middle of your art piece, you'll skip using them there. Use clamps to hold your pieces in place until the glue dries, or just set a heavy object on top to serve as a clamp (see image 7).

12 If there are any boards out of alignment, nail them to their neighboring slat to hold them into place. If you nail down toward the bottom of the piece, once hung those nails will be hidden from the normal range of sight (see image 8).

13 Let the glue dry overnight.

14 Sand the entire piece if desired.

IMAGE 8

chapter 3
around the house

In this chapter, you'll find projects that are the perfect addition to any home in need of a little rustic, unique goodness. Adding items made out of pallet slats in certain areas of your home is a great way to infuse your personal style in small (or large, if you prefer) doses throughout every room. Increase the functionality of a space by adding a unique hook board with vintage knobs or a full-length mirror. Or just bring some beauty to a boring old bookcase by lining the back of it with pallet slats in a brick pattern. And if you're feeling extra ambitious, take the same process from the lined bookcase tutorial and expand it to create an entire accent wall lined with pallet slats. I haven't forgotten about your furry friends, either. Add character to the necessary feeding area with a pallet slat feeding station fit for your most beloved family members. Use these specific projects as a guide to get you started in creating items that make your house feel a little more like home.

hook board with repurposed handles

This project really couldn't be any simpler. The most time-consuming part might be picking out the salvaged hardware to use and deciding on their layout on the board. You can often find old hardware at a Habitat for Humanity ReStore, or you might find some on an old furniture piece at a thrift store. I found mine among piles of what seemed to be complete junk in the backyard shed that was left behind when we purchased our house. You just never know where you will find a little treasure. And what a fun way to honor this house when we move on—this little hook board can move with us when we leave. Maybe your grandmother has an old furniture piece with knobs that would be perfect for this project?

1 Cut the slat to your desired length if a full-length slat is too long for your space.

2 Use the palm sander to sand the pallet slat thoroughly. Start with the medium–grit sandpaper and finish with the fine-grit sandpaper.

3 Decide on the placement of your hooks and mark holes where you will drill pilot holes for screwing in each hook. You could measure for more perfect spacing, but there is nothing wrong with the eyeball method either (see image 1).

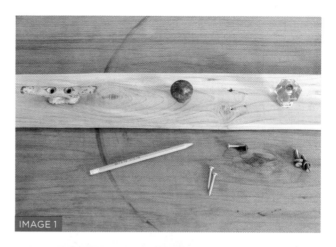

IMAGE 1

4 A ⅛" drill bit should be the right size to drill pillow holes for most hooks/hardware screws but double-check the size of your screws to make sure. The size of your pilot holes should be slightly smaller than the size of your screws, so use the screws as a gauge when picking your drill bit. Drill holes through each mark (see image 2).

5 If you have hooks that don't have screws, apply a strong adhesive to the back side of your hooks and use clamps to hold them in place until the glue dries.

IMAGE 2

6 Voilà, you're done! A couple of 2" nails right through the pallet slat work well to hang it onto hardwood surfaces. If you're hanging it on drywall, you will want to use screws with anchors for enough support.

Tip!!!

A pallet slat with interesting color combinations or unique markings would be a good fit for this project. Look for one that provides visual interest—maybe the wood grain has interesting lines or there are knots creating a fun look.

shoe organizer

part 2: project tutorials

Can we talk for a minute about one of the biggest organization dilemmas to ever show its face in the world of home storage? The dreaded "bottom of the closet." Dun dun dun. Most closets have a plethora of space along the floor, which for me only serves as a gathering place for a mishmash of everything that doesn't otherwise have a designated home. And the shoes! I've tried baskets and bins and lining them up neatly in rows along the closet floor. But what a waste of vertical space.

Here's a really simple shoe-organizing solution that may just change your world . . . or, at least change your closet. This tutorial makes two separate, stackable organizing shelves, and this project can be easily customized depending on how many shoes you have and if you have more of the high-heel variety. Regarding length: The pallet slats I used were only 38″ long but I've seen slats as long as 48″. You could also line up two shelf sections end to end to make a longer line of shoes. Just be sure to support any long sections with support pieces in the middle to prevent sagging over time. Regarding height: You could use a 2×6 or 2×8 board instead of the pallet support boards for additional height if you don't have the same selection of flip-flops I seem to have acquired. As with any project, sanding it down is always a nice touch for a smoother finish, but for this particular project I didn't find it necessary.

INVESTMENT: no money and less than an hour; it actually might *save* you time in the long run since you won't be searching for your shoes amidst other closet randomness, so I guess you could say this project pays you

SUPPLIES
- 6 pallet slats of equal length and thickness
- 2 support boards of equal width
- 24 (1⅛″) screws
- shoes

TOOLS
- tape measure
- miter or handsaw
- cordless drill

supplies needed to make a shoe organizer

IMAGE 1

IMAGE 2

1 Lay 2 sets of 3 pallet slats side by side and measure the width of each set of 3 (see image 1). Cracked or broken slats will work fine for this project—those imperfections are easily hidden facing the back of your closet and under shoes.

2 Use your miter or handsaw to cut 4 pieces of the pallet support boards to the measurements from the previous step.

3 Line up the cut support boards edge side up perpendicular with each end of your sets of 3 slats, and use your cordless drill to attach them with 1⅛" screws. Screw into the holes left when you removed the nails from the pallet slats when dismantling them from the pallet—this will prevent additional cracking (see image 2). Or you can drill new pilot holes if you prefer.

4 If your closet is anything like mine, now might be a good time to clear out anything on the floor and give it a quick and thorough dusting before you put your new organizer in there.

Tip!!!

Before you start this project, gather your shoe collection to gauge the best height and size requirements for this project. How tall is your tallest heel? How long are your shoes? Make this organizer the dimensions that will best fit both your shoes and your closet.

pallet slat-backed bookcase

SUPPLIES

- enough pallet slats to cover your surface area (I used 32 (9¼"-long) pieces of pallet slats)
- medium-grit sandpaper
- wood glue
- painter's tape
- ⅝" nails (optional)
- varnish or wood sealer (optional)

TOOLS

- tape measure
- miter or handsaw
- palm sander (optional)
- table saw
- hammer or nail gun (optional)
- paintbrush (optional—for applying varnish or sealer)

This project is an easy way to bring some extra character to any bookcase, hutch, shelving, or other piece of furniture you have with a boring back. Many nice-looking pieces of furniture come with a plain, ¼"-thick piece of plywood, known as lauan, for a backing. This project, using pallet slats laid in a brick pattern, will even add some pizzazz to an entire accent wall. (Feel free to picture me right here with jazz hands.)

If your bookcase or hutch has removable shelves, make sure they will still fit after the added thickness of the pallet slat backing. You may need to run the shelves through a table saw to cut them down to fit. If the shelves aren't removable, you could instead add the pallet slat pattern above and below each shelf. For this tutorial, I cut my slats into pieces that were 9¼" long because that measurement worked well with the width of my hutch. Four full 9¼" pieces fit along one row. You can use this exact measurement and just make adjustment cuts at the end of each row to make each piece fit with your piece of furniture, or measure the width of your own piece and divide it by 4 and use that measurement.

Here's a look at my hutch before—a little ho-hum if you ask me.

before: boring hutch

1 Use your tape measure to measure the surface area you are going to cover with pallet slats and determine how long you want to cut each pallet slat. (The hutch in this project is 37″ wide, with the pallet slats cut to length so 4 pieces fit per row and enough pieces were cut to fill the height of this hutch at 30″ tall.)

2 Use a miter or handsaw to cut all of your pieces to size. A time-saving tip: When making a number of short cuts with your miter saw that are all the same length, make a pencil mark right on your saw and line up each piece to cut with that mark; that way you don't have to measure each individual piece.

3 Use your palm sander and medium-grit sandpaper to sand each individual piece. Run the sandpaper right along the corners of each cut piece to give them a little bit of a rounded corner.

4 To create the brick pattern, lay your cut pallet slat pieces on the ground in rows. Lay 4 pieces in 1 row end to end, and then use 3 pieces to start the next row with the end of each slat piece ending in the middle of the slat piece of the row below it. Continue this pattern for each row. You will need to make additional cuts to complete the brick pattern with smaller pieces at each end of every other row (see image 1).

5 Use a table saw to rip any row as necessary for your design to fit the height of your bookshelf. For example, my hutch measures 30″ high but my slat pattern measured 31¼″. I chose to rip ¾″ off the bottom and top rows so they would be similar heights. Another option is to make any necessary cuts on the last row only (see image 2).

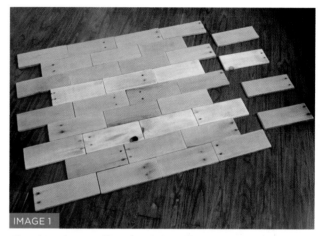

IMAGE 1

the slats shown off to the right will get cut in half to complete that row

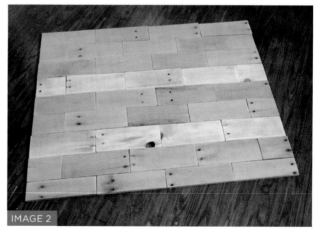

IMAGE 2

the bottom row has been ripped to a height that will fit the hutch

project continued on next page

6   One row at a time, run a bead of glue on the back of each pallet slat piece and then adhere it to the back of your furniture (see images 3 and 4).

7   For additional support as the glue dries, use painter's tape to secure every few rows in place (see image 5).

8   When you get to the last row, measure the distance to the top of your piece and double-check that your last row of slats will indeed fit. Make any additional cuts as needed (see image 6).

9   Wrap a paper towel around a knife and wipe away any glue that starts to drip in between the slats. (The glue will dry clear, but it's nice to try to avoid any drips.) You may need to repeat this step every few minutes depending on how heavy-handed you were with the glue.

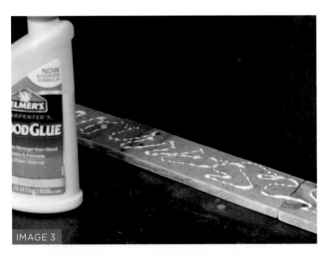

IMAGE 3

IMAGE 4

IMAGE 5

IMAGE 6

10   If desired, add ⅝″ nails with a hammer or nail gun from the backside of your book-shelf for additional support. Use longer nails if the back of your bookcase is thicker than ¼″.

11   Let the glue dry overnight.

12   If desired, apply varnish or sealer.

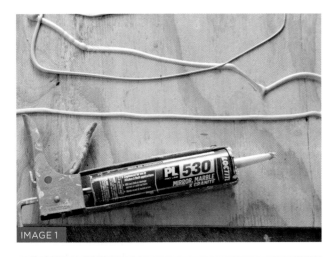

IMAGE 1

IMAGE 2

IMAGE 3

1 Prepare the frame boards by distressing them to your liking. Check out the detailed instructions for making new wood look old in Chapter 7. Bonus points if you scored some reclaimed wood for this project; that makes me officially jealous.

2 Use your tape measure to measure the size of your mirror.

3 Add 11″ to both the height and width of your mirror measurement and mark that measurement on the plywood. This will leave your plywood big enough for a 5½″ frame around all sides of your mirror.

4 Use your circular or table saw to cut the plywood to size.

5 Apply mirror adhesive to the plywood avoiding the 5½″ from each edge for the frame (see image 1).

6 Adhere your mirror to the plywood and let it cure according to the adhesive directions. Depending on the size of your mirror, an extra set of hands to help maneuver the mirror into place could be helpful here.

7 With your miter saw, cut your frame boards out of the 1×6s. Miter the corners 45° on the flat side and make your cuts so the length on the shorter side of each cut board is the same length as the dimensions of your mirror.

8 Adhere the frame boards to the plywood around your mirror with wood glue (see image 2) and let dry overnight. It wouldn't hurt to use clamps or just lay heavy objects on top to ensure the boards are flat while the glue dries (see image 3).

9 When the glue is dry, wipe the wood and mirror clean if necessary and hang with hooks and wire made to hold the weight of your project, or simply lean against a wall.

Tip!!!

Depending on the size of your mirror, you might be able to get both of the horizontal pieces (for the top and bottom of the frame) out of a single 1×6 that is 6' long. When cutting your mitered corners, flip your boards over on your saw to use the previously mitered cuts and save wood.

rustic wooden crate

I am always immediately drawn to those old, rustic crates that you can find in many antique shops. But then I am usually instantly turned off by the price. There's no doubt that a fun history can add to the value of a piece, if it in some way has meaning to you. Maybe it's from a local farmers' market or an old company you know and love. But if it's the look you're going for, luckily these little crates are pretty easy to make. And they can be really handy for so many things and make a fun accent piece when layered into home decor. A wooden crate would be perfect to hold kindling and firewood for your fireplace or filled with a few spare pillows nestled near your sofa.

This crate is easy to customize based on the selection of pallet slats you have available. Get creative! I liked the look of the two narrow slats flanking the one wider slat in the middle, but develop a design that you love and run with it. Or, maybe you'd prefer a solid-sided crate? A couple of years ago I made a solid-sided crate and used it to store our canned goods in our tiny little kitchen. She even has a top with a handle made out of driftwood.

INVESTMENT: a couple of hours and the cost of a few ¾" square dowels

SUPPLIES

‣ 4 narrow pallet slats, cut 19" long

‣ 4 narrow pallet slats, cut 12" long

‣ 2 wide pallet slats, cut 19" long

‣ 2 wide pallet slats, cut 12" long

‣ 4 (¾") square dowels, cut 15" long

‣ 1 sheet ¾" plywood for the bottom of the crate, measuring 17¾" × 12"

‣ medium-grit sandpaper

‣ wood glue

‣ 1" nails

TOOLS

‣ tape measure

‣ miter or handsaw

‣ palm sander (optional)

‣ hammer or nail gun

‣ small level or wood shim to use as a spacer

pallet slat crate; for the full tutorial please visit *http://thespacebetween blog.net/2012/04/10/pallet-wood-kitchen-crate*

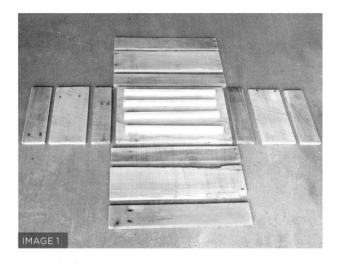

IMAGE 1

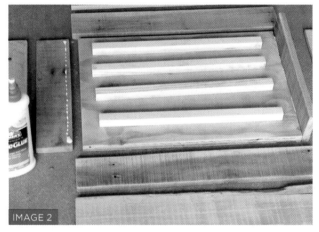

IMAGE 2

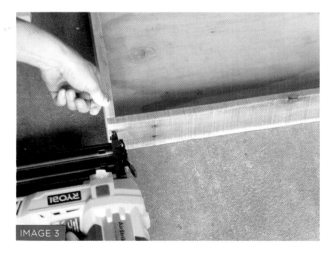

IMAGE 3

IMAGE 4

1   Use a miter or handsaw to make all of the cuts. Use your palm sander and medium-grit sandpaper to sand each piece individually before anything is attached (see image 1).

2   Running a bead of glue at each connection as you go, use 1″ nails and a hammer or nail gun to attach the 2 bottom end pieces to the center bottom piece of plywood (see image 2). Next, attach the 2 bottom side pieces.

3   Attach the tops of those slats to each other with 1 more nail per corner (see image 3).

4   Attach the ¾″ square dowel vertical corner pieces by running a bead of wood glue in each corner and using 2 nails in both sides of each corner (see image 4).

5   Running a bead of glue at each attachment, secure the next layer of side pallet slats. To attach the rows of pallet slats an equal distance apart, cut a shim piece out of scrap wood to use as a spacer. This will ensure each slat is attached at exactly the same

height in that row (see image 5). Or you could use a small level for each section. Attach the end slats to the corner pieces with 2–4 nails per end. Next, attach the side slats in the same manner (see image 6).

6 Attach the top layer the same way (see images 7 and 8).

7 Now the only decision is what to put in it.

IMAGE 5

IMAGE 6

first attach the slats on the end of your crate and then line up the slats on each side

IMAGE 7

don't worry if your vertical corner pieces don't line up perfectly right away with the end of the slats you are connecting horizontally; you might need to "persuade" each piece a little to set them in the exact spot you want at each end of the crate

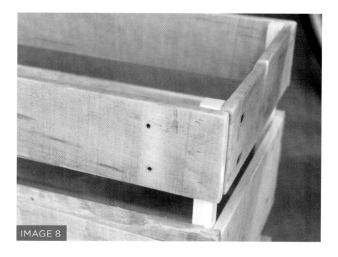

IMAGE 8

Tip!!!

Check out Chapter 4, Holidays and Entertaining, to see how to use this crate as a storage spot for gifts and decor for the holidays.

pet feeding station

Can we all just agree that pets are awesome? In our house Marley and Mico, affectionately dubbed "the girls," are just as much a part of our family as the humans we surround ourselves with. They don't ever like to stray too far away from what we're doing and they sure know how to show some unconditional love. Hoping to fall short of being the crazy dog lady who tries to teach them how to sit nicely at the table (Who would pick up my food scraps below?), this little pet feeding station spruces up the necessary food bowl corner in any home. If you have larger dogs, you could easily add some legs so yours sits at just the right height for your pets' dining pleasure. This is a good project to use scrap pallet slats left over from other projects.

And, if your pet is a messy eater, this might not be the right project for you. Keep in mind all of the cautions and information about pallet wood in Part 1 and consider all of the information very carefully before making this project. There are many food-grade sealers on the market; after some research, you should be able to find one that you are comfortable with.

INVESTMENT: a couple of hours or less and the cost of the bowls if you don't already have them on hand

SUPPLIES

- pallet slats to create the desired rectangle shape
- 2 bowls with a lip around the edge
- 4 pallet support boards
- 2" nails
- wood glue
- 1¼" nails
- medium-grit sandpaper
- food-grade wood sealer

TOOLS

- straightedge
- miter or handsaw
- tape measure
- hammer or nail gun
- speed square
- sawhorses
- cordless drill
- ½" or larger drill bit
- jigsaw
- clamp
- palm sander (optional)

1 Lay out enough pallet slats side by side underneath your bowls so there is a couple of inches of a wood edge around each bowl. Also, make sure the space between the bowls is not a space between two slats (see image 1).

2 Use a straightedge to mark where to cut each slat to your desired rectangle size (see image 2).

3 Use a miter or handsaw to cut the slats to size.

4 Measure the length and width of your now-cut rectangle. Let the width of your pallet slats determine the overall measurement of your project (see image 3). This will save you the extra work of deciding on a measurement first and creating extra cuts to make the slats fit that size.

5 Cut the support boards to size: First, cut 2 the exact length of your pallet slat rectangle. Next,

IMAGE 1

make sure a slat, and not a space between slats, runs between the bowls

IMAGE 3

IMAGE 2

IMAGE 4

line those up with each edge and measure inside them to get the measurement for the other 2 support boards that will run the width of the rectangle (see image 4).

6 Use a hammer or nail gun to attach your 4 support boards together with 2″ nails, 2–4 nails per corner (see image 5).

7 Run a bead of wood glue along the top edge and attach the pallet slats to the top (see image 6). Add 1¼″ nails with your hammer or nail gun.

8 Place bowls upside down in desired location and trace (see image 7). *Do not cut this line!* It is only a guide.

9 Mark the center of the circle you have already traced (see image 8).

IMAGE 5

IMAGE 7

IMAGE 6

IMAGE 8

even with the most accurate measurements, which I don't ever claim to have (sometimes that little tape measure just will not cooperate—am I right?), getting old, weathered wood to line up perfectly straight can be a challenge; embrace the imperfection—it's part of the charm

project continued on next page

10 Measure the depth of the lip on your bowls (mine are ⅜″; see image 9).

11 Use a speed square and a pencil to create a makeshift compass and create a cut line *inside* the bowl edge line (see image 10). If that proves difficult—and trust me, it does—I'm not above eye-balling it, either. This cut is going to be hidden under the lip of the bowls in the long run. Give it a shot. As long as you're *inside* the bowl edge mark, you're good to go.

12 Set your project on a pair of sawhorses so you don't incidentally drill into something you love. Drill a ½″ hole anywhere along the inside edge of your cut lines (see image 11).

13 Cross your fingers and hope that your line is in the right spot—just kidding, kind of.

14 Start with your blade in your newly drilled hole and jigsaw out the holes for the bowls (see image 12).

IMAGE 9

IMAGE 11

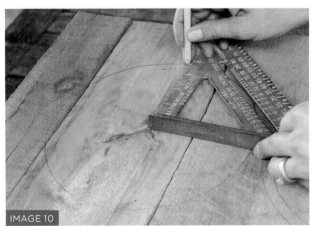
IMAGE 10

line up the corner of your speed square with your center mark and as you move the square in a circle around the center point, mark your cut line the appropriate distance inside your bowl edge line

IMAGE 12

15 Check the fit of the bowls and make additional cuts as necessary. While jigsawing, use a clamp to hold your project steady if the cut pallet slats start to shake (see image 13).

16 Using 1¼" nails and your hammer or a nail gun, attach the cut slats to the slat beside it for additional support (see image 14).

17 Use your palm sander with medium-grit sandpaper to sand the entire project.

18 Seal the project with a food-grade wood sealer.

Tip!!!

A couple of alternative options to create the circle you need to cut out for this project are 1) look for a bowl, plate, or any other circular item that is the same size as the diameter of the bowl without the lip overhang. Can you believe we had nothing? Or 2) use the nail, string, and pencil method we used to make the Rustic Wood Clock in Chapter 2.

IMAGE 13

IMAGE 14

chapter 4
holidays and entertaining

Who doesn't like to throw a party every now and again? In this chapter, you'll find items intended to enhance your holiday celebrations and entertaining endeavors. But what you may also find are some items you'll want to keep around throughout the entire year. Many of these ideas, customized here to represent a holiday idea, can easily transition to a project that is not defined by one specific celebration. I'd love to see how you personalize any of the ideas in this chapter and throughout the book. Give me a shout at the blog, *http://thespacebetweenblog.net*—and share all of your unique variations.

easy peasy star

Sometimes the simplest projects make the biggest impression. This little star—which literally takes minutes to complete—is one of those projects. As soon as she was complete, I knew she would look fabulous with a few strings of lights and some greenery, and she would end up the star of our holiday decor. (Pun, what pun?) She's just so festive and bright and just the right touch of rustic mixed with a few glowing baubles. How fun would these stars be strung with lights and hung outside each of your house windows instead of wreaths? *So* fun. That is the answer.

But this star could easily move around to different areas of your home throughout the year (Fourth of July?) as an anchor in many a vignette. She can even hold her own on a little ledge; no fancy accessories required. If you'd like a more refined look for your star, you could sand each slat or embellish her with your favorite color of paint. But she's not too shabby in her simple, rustic glory either.

INVESTMENT: a few minutes to make and then an immeasurable number of minutes gazing at your simplistically perfect creation (seriously, that is going to happen, especially at night wrapped with lights—you just wait!)

SUPPLIES

‣ 5 pallet slats of the same length and width

‣ 7 (1⅛") screws

TOOL

‣ cordless drill

this simple star looks great leaning on any ledge or mantel

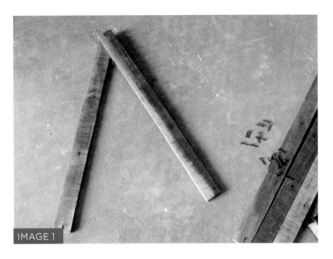

IMAGE 1

IMAGE 2

IMAGE 3

1 Lay your 5 pallet slats in the shape of a star (see images 1–4). There will be a bit of a gap where the tip of #3 and #5 will be attached, but it's nothing a little muscle can't overcome when it comes time to screw that corner together.

IMAGE 4

2 Now it's time to connect them. First, use a screw to connect the corner of #1 to #3 (see image 5); then #2 to #1; and then #4 to #1, not in the corner but where #4 overlaps #1 (see image 6). Next, connect the corner of #4 to #2, then #5 into #4.

3 Finally, you'll screw #5 into #3. Here's a close-up of the gap between slats #3 and #5 (see image 7). I just used a little extra pressure on the slat with my foot while screwing it in from the front, and to give it extra security, I added an additional screw from the back side of that corner as well. Easy peasy, right?!

IMAGE 5

connecting the star points

IMAGE 6

IMAGE 7

painted silhouette

INVESTMENT: less than the time it takes you to watch a full-length holiday movie

SUPPLIES

- 3 pallet slats measuring about 11″ wide when laid side by side, cut 14″ long
- 2 (1×2) wood pieces, cut 6″ long
- wood glue
- 4 (1″) nails (optional)
- silhouette image
- paint
- medium-grit sandpaper (optional)

TOOLS

- tape measure
- miter or handsaw
- clamps or a heavy object
- hammer or nail gun (optional)
- scissors or X-Acto knife
- paintbrush
- palm sander (optional) (optional)

We've come to the point of making our second silhouette art option (you can find the first one in Chapter 2). This one is the perfect project for a little nighttime crafting while watching your favorite holiday movies that you've already seen a million times, and that you can recite the lyrics and dialogue to on-command—but have to watch every holiday season anyway, because they're awesome. You can make this craft as large or as small as you like. I chose to outline the painted image in white, and I ended up using a clear wax to finish it off and give it just the slightest bit of sheen and a little extra glimmer for the holidays. I fell just one step short of beglittering (you know, like bedazzling only with glitter) her, but that might just add the right amount of glitz to this rustic little piece.

1 Use a miter or handsaw to cut the slats and 1×2s to length (see image 1).

2 Lay the 1×2s vertically on their flat sides and run a bead of wood glue on each.

3 Lay the slats horizontally on top of the 1×2s (see image 2). Clamp or weigh down with a heavy object and let dry overnight. If you don't want to use glue, use a hammer or nail gun to secure together with the nails.

4 Find and print image.

5 Cut out the image with your scissors or X-Acto knife, and then trace it onto the pallet slats.

6 Paint the image onto the pallet slats (see image 3).

7 Sand if desired. (Sanding over the painted area will give it a distressed look.)

Tip!!!

You can find finishing wax at most home improvement stores, and it is available in light or dark options. When applied with a natural-fiber brush and buffed smooth, the wax adds a nice sheen and softness to your project. Wax works great on small craft projects as well as large furniture pieces.

IMAGE 1

IMAGE 2

IMAGE 3

rustic advent calendar

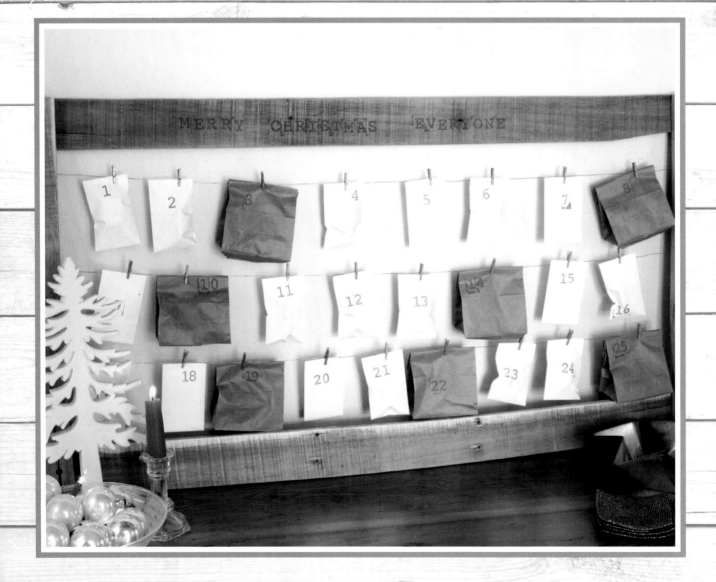

I've always loved the idea of a unique way to count down the days until Christmas. There's just something about building up the excitement one day at a time with a reminder of how close you're getting to the big day. A couple of years ago, I turned a branch I found on the side of the road into a way to count down the days by doing random acts of kindness. (You can find the full tutorial on the blog, complete with some kindness ideas, *http://thespacebetweenblog .net/2012/11/12/countdown-to-christmas/*.) And there's no reason why you couldn't fill each of the treat bags for this project with a random act of kindness idea. Or whatever little treat you know your loved ones will enjoy. Children could even help with some parts of this project—talk about a fun way to kick off the holiday season!

INVESTMENT: the cost of the treat bags and clips and the time it takes to get into the holiday spirit

SUPPLIES

‣ 2 full slats
‣ 1 full slat, cut in half
‣ 8 (1⅛") screws
‣ medium-grit sandpaper (optional)
‣ 6 eye hooks
‣ wire or string
‣ 25 small bags
‣ 25 small clips or clothespins

TOOLS

‣ miter or handsaw
‣ cordless drill
‣ palm sander (optional)
‣ drill bit, size based on the size of the screw end of your eye hooks
‣ needle-nose pliers
‣ marker or rubber stamp set (optional)

supplies needed to make a rustic advent calendar

1 Create a rectangle with the full-length slats and half-length slats; line up each corner of the rectangle with the vertical half-length slats on the top of the full-length slats running horizontally. Use your cordless drill to attach with 2 screws per corner (see image 1). You could use pallet slat scraps for the half-length or use a handsaw or miter saw to cut a slat to size.

2 Use your palm sander and medium-grit sandpaper to smooth each slat if desired.

3 Flip the rectangle over and use the height of your treat bags as a guide to measure where to add your eye hooks. How many rows you make will depend on the length of your pallet slats and the size of your treat bags (see image 2).

4 To help get the eye hooks started, use your cordless drill fitted with the drill bit to drill in barely 1/16" to give a defined spot to start screwing the hooks in straight (see image 3).

IMAGE 1

IMAGE 2

IMAGE 3

IMAGE 4

5 Screw in your eye hooks. If you have trouble screwing in the eye hooks by hand, needle-nose pliers can help (see image 4).

6 Run your wire or string horizontally between the eye hooks and cut to length (see image 5).

7 Set your assembled wooden rectangle aside and use a marker, rubber stamp set, paint, or whatever you have to number your bags 1–25 (see image 6).

8 Fill your bags with advent treats and hang each from the wire with your small clips or clothespins.

9 Add any other embellishments or messages of the season to the rectangle frame if desired.

Tip!!!

For this project, it is okay if your pallet slats split when you attach with the screws. If you'd like to prevent them from splitting, however, you can always drill pilot holes slightly smaller than the diameter of your screws.

IMAGE 5

IMAGE 6

miniature tabletop tree

INVESTMENT: about an hour of holiday fun time

SUPPLIES

- 2 or 3 pallet slats (using 5 small scrap pallet slat pieces will also work due to the small nature of this craft project)
- medium-grit sandpaper
- 1×2 wood, about as long as you'll want your tree to measure in height
- wood glue
- 1¼" nails

TOOLS

- tape measure
- jigsaw
- speed square
- clamp
- sawhorse
- palm sander (optional)
- heavy object (optional)
- hammer or nail gun

Here's to festive little craft projects that can be made in mere minutes. I actually made a few of these little trees as gifts last year—they were a big hit. This could be a super-fun kids' activity at a holiday or birthday party. Cut and sand the trees ahead of time, then let kids assemble and embellish them with paint or glitter. (Who am I kidding? I want to do that for my next girls' night get-together, but it sounds like it would be fun for kids, too.) These trees are so versatile—they could be a fun addition to your a winter-themed mantel. Scatter them throughout open shelving in your kitchen or put a couple on your guest bathroom vanity for a touch of holiday spirit in every room. This is the perfect project to use up those random pallet slat pieces that aren't really big enough for the other projects but are too big to just throw away.

1 Use your jigsaw to cut a pallet slat into your tree base and trunk pieces. A small square, roughly 3″ × 3″, works well for a base, and a small rectangle, roughly 1½″ × 3″, makes a nice trunk (see image 1). You could also choose to make the base another shape if you prefer.

2 Lay 3 slat pieces side by side and use a speed square and pencil to mark angles on each slat to create a tree shape. The top of the tree should come to a point, the top of the next slat should start inside the bottom of the slat above it by about ¾″, and the bottom slat should also be indented about ¾″ (see image 2).

3 Use your jigsaw with the wood pieces clamped to a work surface for additional stability and cut each slat along your marks (see image 3).

4 Use your palm sander and medium-grit sandpaper to sand each piece.

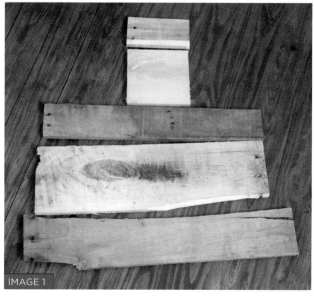

the top piece is the trunk and the square below it is the base piece; the other pallet pieces will get marked and cut to create the tree shape in the next steps

IMAGE 2

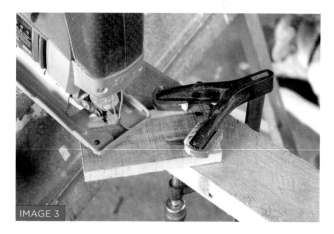

IMAGE 3

project continued on next page

IMAGE 4

IMAGE 5

5 Use your jigsaw to cut your 1×2 to length. You want it to be about 2″ shorter than the height of all of your cut tree sections together. Run a bead of glue on the flat side of 1×2 to attach each of the 3 tree slats and the trunk. Start with the bottom of the trunk lined up with the bottom on the 1×2 (see image 4).

6 Let the glue dry overnight. You could use a cinder block or other heavy object to "clamp" down the slats while the glue dries. You may need to support the corners of the cinder block with scrap wood to prevent tipping over.

7 To install the base, nail straight up through the base piece into the trunk and 1×2 support (see image 5).

Tip!!!

I tried making these small trees with different width pallet slats and it looked a little wonky for my liking. The uniform slats give it a good tree shape and the variety in the color and textures of the wood add just the right element of quirk for my liking.

American flag

I love the look of a rustic, wooden flag. We have had a few cloth flags over the years that have gotten tattered and torn after years of blowing in the wind, and I thought that instead of investing in another one it was time to make one out of wood that would prove to be more durable. This project turned out to be the perfect example of how things don't always go right the first time around. Something about math and division and fifty stars in one little blue box gave my brain a run for its money. But, all's well that ends well, even if I did have to buy more paint to compensate for my shaky math skills.

INVESTMENT: a little patriotism and an afternoon; if you don't have craft paint on hand, that will be your only cost

SUPPLIES

- 6 pallet slats, about 44" long
- 1 pallet support board, cut into 2 pieces 22" long
- 24 (1⅛") screws
- red, white, and blue paint
- medium-grit sandpaper
- potato
- paper towel
- dark wax (optional)

TOOLS

- tape measure
- miter or handsaw
- cordless drill
- craft paint brushes
- 4' straightedge
- palm sander (optional)
- knife (to cut the potato)
- natural-fiber brush (optional—to apply the wax)

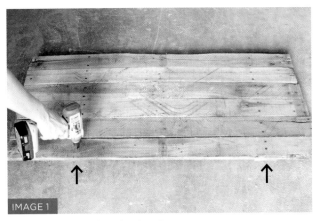

length, 44″; and height, 23½″

IMAGE 2

IMAGE 3

1 Use your miter or handsaw to cut your pallet slats and support boards to size. The support boards should be slightly shorter than the height of your pallet slats when laid side by side. You can find many resources for the exact dimensions of the American flag online. As a guide, a traditional American flag is almost twice as wide as it is high. For this project, I am using a loose interpretation of those dimensions. They are close enough that anyone looking at the flag will know it is pretty darn close, but I definitely wouldn't want to be judged for accuracy.

2 Lay the pallet slats side by side horizontally over the 2 support boards that are laid vertically and use your cordless drill to attach with 1⅛″ screws; use 2 screws per slat per support board (see image 1).

3 Next, we're going to measure the blue box on the flag. A basic guide is that the width of the blue box is about ¾ of the measurement of the total height of the flag. So, since my flag is just over 23″ high, I measured 18″ across the top (18 is *about* ¾ of 23). The height of the blue box is just over half of the total height of the whole flag. Since my flag is 6 pallet slats tall, I made the blue box slightly bigger than 3 slats tall.

4 Paint the area for the blue box and then paint the remainder of the flag white. Let dry.

5 Measure 13 equal horizontal stripes, and mark them with the 4′ straightedge (see image 2). Paint the top stripe and every other stripe red (see image 3). You will end up with 7 red stripes and 6 white stripes.

6 Sand the entire piece with medium-grit sandpaper to give it a distressed look.

7 Now we'll make a stamp out of that potato. Carve a star shape out of the potato with your knife (see image 4). (If you have a star stencil or rubber stamp, you could use that instead.) Coat the star with white paint. Stamp stars in the blue box, alternating between rows of 6 stars and rows of 5, ending up with 50 total (see image 5). Use a paper towel to wipe excess paint off the potato as you go. Now, if you happen to line up your stars wrong, not leaving yourself enough room for all 50 stars, you may need to reapply blue paint and start the potato stamping over. Not that I would know.

8 To kick up the distressed look of your project a few notches, use a natural-fiber brush to apply a dark wax if desired (see image 6). A little tip about the wax: a little goes a very long way, especially with dark wax. Start with a little bit and work into it, adding more to produce a more distressed look. Also, you may have noticed how bright the red paint looked when I was painting. If you do plan to finish with a dark wax, start with brighter paint than you think you want—the wax will tone it down and give it an entirely different look when you are done. (Find more details about waxing and other finishing touches in Chapter 7.)

IMAGE 4

making a potato stamp

IMAGE 5

IMAGE 6

Tip!!!

You may need to play around with the layout of your pallet slats before you finalize their placement. Some lay more closely lined-up with certain slats than others. And this is a great project to use slats that have splits and cracks in them if you like the rustic look; the slight variations add to the rustic nature of the art piece.

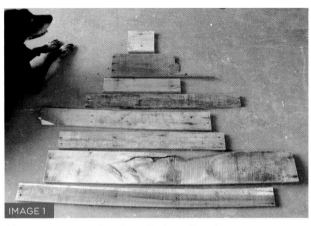

IMAGE 1

the puppy supervisor is entirely optional

IMAGE 2

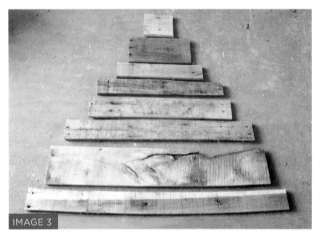

IMAGE 3

1   Lay out pallet slats to create the tree shape you like (see image 1).

2   Use a speed square or straightedge and pencil to mark each slat at the desired length to create the tree shape (see image 2).

3   Use a miter or handsaw to cut each slat on the marks to create your tree shape (see image 3).

4   Set the pallet slats aside and assemble the tree trunk and base. Use a miter or handsaw to cut 1 support board into 3 pieces: one 15" long and two 7" long. Set them in an X shape for the base (see image 4).

5   Use a cordless drill and the flat corner L brackets to secure the base pieces together with the screws provided in the L bracket packaging (see image 5).

6   Add the self-adhesive felt pads to the bottom of the base (see image 6) for two reasons:

1.   to protect your floors when displaying your tree
2.   so the X base sits flat even with the corner L brackets attached

7   Lay your pallet slats in the shape of your tree to determine how tall of a trunk you need (see image 7). Use a miter or handsaw to cut the remaining pallet support board to size if necessary. (If you want a particularly tall tree, you could purchase a 2×4 to use for the trunk instead of using a pallet support board.)

IMAGE 4

IMAGE 5

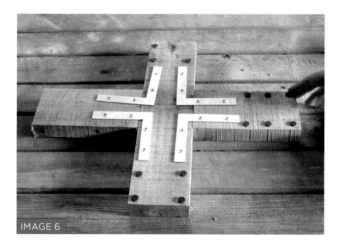

IMAGE 6

IMAGE 7

project continued on next page

8 Place the support board you are using for the trunk on a sawhorse and secure your pocket hole jig to the board with a clamp. Use your cordless drill to drill 3 pocket holes in the back of the board (see image 8). If you don't have a pocket hole jig to drill the pocket holes, you can use L brackets to attach the trunk to the X base (see image 9).

9 Use the cordless drill to attach the trunk to the base through the pocket holes with 1¼" screws (see image 10).

10 Lay the trunk on a step, or anything with a similar height as the back of the X base so the trunk is laying horizontally. Lay out the slats for an approximate design (see image 11).

11 Attach each slat to the trunk with 2 (1⅛") screws per slat using your cordless drill. You could use a tape measure to ensure the slats are centered, or just eyeball it, my preferred method in most cases.

IMAGE 8

IMAGE 10

IMAGE 9

IMAGE 11

12 Decorate and enjoy (see image 12).

13 Using a palm sander to smooth out any rough edges on your pallet slats is always a good way to finish off a project. Or . . . paint, stain, and distress a few slats for a more colorful look (see image 13) if desired.

Tip!!!

For any project you might want to disassemble at any point consider using screws instead of wood glue and nails. Now you can easily take out the screws and store this tree out of sight throughout the year.

IMAGE 12

IMAGE 13

tray with mitered corners

A stylish tray can work well in many spaces for anything from a place to stack your magazines on your coffee table or ottoman to a serving station for plates and glassware at your next dinner party. The vintage handles add another element of detail to this otherwise straightforward design. If you wanted to add a bit more flair, you could incorporate the herringbone pattern from the Herringbone Coffee Table tutorial in Chapter 6 or an arrow design, similar to the drawers on the Night Stand with Arrow Detail in Chapter 6. The gray patina of these specific wood slats gave just the right touch of a rustic feel that only a light sanding was necessary, only to remove any loose splinters. Be on the lookout for pallets with wood tones that you are drawn to—those will work well for projects you want to keep unsanded.

INVESTMENT: a couple of hours and the cost of some old handles

SUPPLIES

- 3 pallet slats, cut 21" long
- 1 pallet slat at least 50" long to miter cut for the tray edges
- scrap wood support pieces ⅝" thick or less, about 8" long
- medium-grit sandpaper
- wood glue
- 1" nails
- self-adhesive felt pads (optional)
- 1 set of handles (optional)
- 2 drill bits, one that is slightly bigger than the threaded end of the screws and a second that is slightly bigger than the head of the screws for your handles (optional)

TOOLS

- tape measure
- miter saw
- table saw
- palm sander (optional)
- hammer or nail gun
- cordless drill (optional)

1. Lay the 3 slats measuring 21″ long side by side; they will end up being the bottom of your tray.

2. Measure the width of these 3 slats. This measurement is the length of the shorter side of your mitered corners, the side that will face the inside of the tray.

3. Miter one end of the slat for the edges at 45° angle on the edge side of the piece of wood. Remember the side of the board facing the inside of the tray needs to be shorter than the side of the board facing out from the tray.

4. Measure from the shorter side of the cut angle to the length of your measurement from step 2 and mark it (see image 1).

5. Cut an opposing 45° cut at your mark. Be sure to cut the angle in the right direction, with longer edges on the same side of the board and the shorter edges on the other side.

Tip!!!

Saw blades measure ⅛″ thick—keep this in mind when lining up your saw blade with your marks. Line up the blade just outside your lines. You can always take another sliver off, but I still haven't figured out how to add wood back when my cuts are too short. Angled cuts can be particularly tricky to line up, so go slowly and err on the side of making the cut too long. There's no harm in needing to shave off a little bit with a few extra cuts.

6. Repeat this process for the length of the tray as well.

7. Run both of the edge pieces through a table saw, ripping it in half lengthwise and creating the 4 total edge pieces you need for the tray (see image 2). You can choose to leave the edge pieces full-width if you don't have a table saw. In that case, just be sure to miter cut 2 pieces at each of your measurements (the length and width of your tray—4 pieces total, 2 of each measurement).

IMAGE 1

IMAGE 2

line up your tape measure with the short end of the miter cut

8 Use a palm sander and medium- or fine-grit sandpaper to lightly sand all pallet wood pieces before assembly.

9 Lay 2 support pieces on their flat sides about 6–10" apart and run a bead of glue along the top of them.

10 Attach the 3 slats to the 2 support pieces with 1" nails to create the bottom of your tray (see image 3). Use 2 nails per slat per support piece (12 total). Add the self-adhesive felt pads to the bottom of each support piece if desired.

IMAGE 3

IMAGE 4

11 One at a time, attach each edge piece. Add 1 nail per edge all the way around to get each mitered corner lined up as much as possible while leaving flexibility to maneuver each piece into place (see image 4). You could also run a bead of glue if desired.

12 When everything is lined up as closely as possible, add 2 or 3 nails to each side and secure each mitered corner with an additional nail (see image 5).

13 Now you have a fine little tray to use for anything from a place to stack books on your coffee table to a base for a nice bowl and accessories on a sofa table. If desired, you could stop here. But, for something a little extra, I thought adding handles would be a fun touch. And since the set I used came out of our backyard shed they weren't any added expense. (The Habitat for Humanity ReStore is a good place to find used items like handles and hardware.)

IMAGE 5

project continued on next page

14 To add the handles, measure to find the center along the edge piece of each end of your tray. You can also eyeball your center based on the center slat in the bottom of your tray.

15 Using the center mark and the handles you are using as a guide, measure for your handle holes and mark (see image 6).

16 Using the screws that go with your handles as a guide, find a drill bit that is slightly bigger than the threaded end of the screw and a second drill bit that is slightly bigger than the head of the screw (see image 7).

17 Make sure your tray is propped up on scrap wood or on a sawhorse so your drill has room to come out below without damaging anything underneath. Drill all the way through your marks with the smaller drill bit (see image 8).

18 Screw the screws all the way into the handle (not attaching it to the wood yet) and place up to the edge of the tray and mark where the

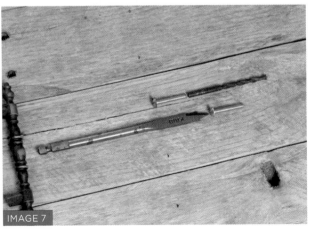

IMAGE 6

IMAGE 7

IMAGE 8

IMAGE 9

head of the screw will be when the handle is attached (see image 9).

19 Flip over your tray and mark on the larger drill bit with painter's tape how far to drill to reach your mark (see image 10).

20 From the bottom side of your tray, very carefully drill straight through the small hole until the painter's tape reaches the wood (see image 11). Make sure you use a nice, sharp drill bit—the sharper the bit, the cleaner the hole it will make.

When you have very little room for error this will give you the greatest opportunity for success.

21 Use the small drill bit to tap the screws into the holes so the threads come out through the top (see images 12 and 13).

22 Line up the threads of the screws with the holes on your handle and use a cordless drill to tighten them securely. Tighten each screw a little at a time to help the threads stay lined up so the handle screws in completely straight. All done!

IMAGE 10

IMAGE 12

IMAGE 11

IMAGE 13

chapter 5
in the yard

In this chapter you will find projects great for the outside of your home and around your yard. A few rustic touches added to even the most modern of designs can add just the right amount of eclectic style to bring your yard from basic to beautiful. As always, feel free to tailor these projects to your specific home and alter measurements or colors to suit your space and preferences.

eclectic directional sign

INVESTMENT: a few nights of stenciling and painting while watching your favorite television shows and the cost of a 4×4 post

SUPPLIES

- pallet slats (the number will depend on how many signs you want to make)
- paint
- 4×4 post (or reclaimed wood post)
- medium-grit sandpaper
- polyurethane
- 1⅛" screws (the number will depend on how many signs you are making)

TOOLS

- tape measure
- miter or handsaw
- letter and number stencils
- small craft paintbrushes
- palm sander (optional)
- cordless drill

Directional signs are pretty popular here in Key West. You see them in random yards of homes and at a variety of different businesses in town. They are measuring the distance to any variety of locations around the world. Since my husband and I move every few years, it seemed like a fun idea to create our own sign to chronicle how far we currently are from the other locations we've lived. It could be fun to make one with the locations of all of your family members, or maybe even all of your dream vacations.

I actually used old fence pickets for my wood in this project. We had just started a fence upgrade in our yard and had them on hand.

1 Decide how many signs you would like to make and use a miter or handsaw to cut your pallet slats to the desired length and shape. Mine are about 30", but none of them is exactly the same. Use your saw to cut pointed ends at one end of each pallet slat.

2 Use a small craft paintbrush to paint your desired locations and distances on each sign (see images 1 and 2). You can use any font, stencil, or free-hand paint strategy that works for you.

3 Paint or stain your 4×4 post if desired.

4 Use your palm sander with medium-grit sandpaper to sand and distress each pallet slat and the 4×4 post if desired.

5 Coat each pallet slat and your 4×4 post with polyurethane to seal if desired.

6 Use a cordless drill to attach each sign to your 4×4 post with 1⅛" screws.

7 To display your new creation, you could either:

- dig a hole and "plant" this piece in a permanent location
- add an X base so it stands alone (see the instructions for making an X base in the Pallet Slat Tree project in Chapter 4)

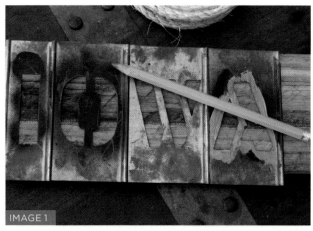

IMAGE 1

I like to first trace the outline and then fill it in with paint

IMAGE 2

after finding an image online, I just traced it and created my own imperfect mile marker zero sign

Tip!!!

To find the mileage from one distance to another, type, for example, "mileage from Key West to Maine" into a search engine.

hanging bed

part 2: project tutorials

This project is inspired by the idea of lounging in a hammock and swinging in the breeze. But have you seen the price of a good hammock these days? If you use a pallet for your base, your only expense is the cost of the rope to hang and then any cushions and pillows you want to add. When determining what to hang your bed from, be sure to check with professionals to make sure it can carry the load of the new bed plus the weight of anyone on it. You might also need to drill holes through something to hang this bed—again, check that you're not compromising the structural integrity of anything before you drill into it. We wouldn't want your relaxing afternoon nap to turn into a collision with the ground below. If you don't have a good spot to hang a pallet bed, you could just lay the pallets right on the ground.

With this project in mind, keep your eyes out for a good-size pallet—one that is approximately twice as long as it is wide would be perfect. You could even ask at different stores to see if they ever receive that size of pallet; maybe they'll set it aside for you.

the first pallet bed I made for our rooftop patio in Curaçao; you can find the full project at *http://thespacebetweenblog.net/2012/06/04/how-to-make-a-pallet-bed/*

INVESTMENT: you don't even have to take a pallet apart for this one, but you will need to buy some rope and cushions; you might need to enlist the help of a friend, but then you can take a nap on your new bed after about an hour of work

SUPPLIES

‣ 1 full pallet about 80" × 40"

‣ 3 (2×4) pieces cut the same length as your pallet

‣ 18 (2½") screws

‣ 40' of ¾" rope, cut into 2 equal sections (the actual length you need will depend on the height of whatever you are hanging your bed from)

‣ painter's tape

TOOLS

‣ tape measure

‣ miter or handsaw

‣ hammer or mallet

‣ cordless drill

‣ 1" drill bit

‣ serrated knife

IMAGE 1

IMAGE 2

you could skip this drilling and just tie the rope around the whole pallet, but these drilled holes will keep the rope in a specific spot

1 Find a pallet your desired size. You won't be taking it apart so look for a pallet with the slats securely attached. If any slats are loose, a few screws work well to reattach them.

2 Use your tape measure to measure the length of your pallet.

3 Use a miter or handsaw to cut all of the 2×4s to that same measurement.

4 Attach a 2×4 to each of the 3 support boards on your pallet to give it the structural integrity it needs to support weight while hanging. You will insert them all from one end and you can nudge them along with a hammer or mallet if necessary. Butt each 2×4 right beside the support boards and attach them with 2½" screws, 5 or 6 per board (see image 1).

5 Starting at the edge of each corner of the pallet, measure 7" in on the long sides of the pallet and drill a 1" hole at each spot through both the support board and the 2×4 (see image 2). You will be making 4 separate holes.

6 Measure the distance down from where you will be hanging your bed to the point in the air you would like your bed to hang. Double that measurement and then add 4'—this is how long you will want to cut your rope. For example, if your measurement is 6' you will want 16' of rope.

7 Measure your rope to the length from step 6. Wrap a piece of painter's tape around the rope at that measurement and use a serrated knife to cut the rope through the painter's tape.

8 Repeat the previous step so you have 2 pieces of rope the same length—for this tutorial, each piece would be 16′ long.

9 Run an end of 1 piece of rope through one of the holes you drilled in your pallet and tie a knot. If you want the knot showing, run the rope so the end is outside of the pallet (see images 3 and 4).

10 Repeat step 9, running the other section of rope through the hole in the other end of the pallet on that same side.

IMAGE 3

11 Run both sections of rope over what you will be hanging your bed from. It is very helpful to have a second set of hands to assist you from here on out.

12 Repeat step 9 with the other ends of each piece of rope, threading them through the holes you drilled on the other side of your pallet. Pull the rope taught so your bed hangs at your desired height before tightening each knot. For a fancier knot you could tie a slip knot—the weight of the bed will pull the knot tight but it will also be easy to loosen if you ever need to move your bed. (Search online for a slip knot tutorial if you'd like to use that option.)

IMAGE 4

Tip!!!

If you have a table saw, you can run each 2×4 through the table saw on the flat side to rip down the width by ⅛″ to make it easier to insert them into your pallet. Even though the hammer or mallet technique with the full-size 2×4 takes a little more effort, it does still work.

13 Trim the rope if necessary and deck out your new bed with cushions, pillows, and puppy blankets.

shutters

A simple set of shutters is an easy way to add a little curb appeal to the front of your home. You don't even need to add them to every single window of your house—consider just making a pair for the windows that can be seen from the street. Depending on the size of your windows, you might actually be able to use pallet slats, but for this tutorial I've used new 1×4s to show that with a little sanding and staining they can end up having the same look as a pallet slat. The tools and supplies list assumes you're making 2 shutters, so multiply everything by 2 for each additional set you'd like to make.

And when it comes to the sizing of window shutters, what will be appropriate for your windows will vary depending on the style of your house and your personal preference. Take a drive around your area and see where your neighbors' shutters line up with their windows. Are they as tall as their window trim? Are they very narrow or do they appear to be about half the width of the entire window? Which style do you like best? These observations will help you determine your specific shutter measurements. Or just wing it and make whatever size you want; there's no hard and fast rule here. Because really, who likes rules? And if you, too, need to use new wood, remember that the actual measurement of a 1×4 is ¾" × 3½".

INVESTMENT: the drying time for the stain and polyurethane could take a few days depending on how many coats you want, but the only cost is the price of the 1×4s and the shutter hardware, assuming you already have wood stain and polyurethane

SUPPLIES

- 1×4s (how many you need and the length will depend on the size of your windows and the style of shutter you choose)
- medium-grit sandpaper
- cotton cloth (for stain application)
- wood stain
- polyurethane
- wood glue
- 1¼" screws
- shutter-hanging hardware (found at most home improvement or hardware stores)

TOOLS

- tape measure
- miter or handsaw
- palm sander (optional)
- paintbrush (for applying polyurethane)
- cordless drill

check out how we accented the shutters on the porch with many upcycled elements at *http://thespacebetweenblog.net/2014/04/17/creating-curb-appeal-front-porch-decorating/*

IMAGE 1

IMAGE 2

IMAGE 3

1 Use your tape measure to measure the height and width of your windows.

2 Use a miter or handsaw to cut your 1×4s to the same length as the height of your windows. How many pieces you need to cut will depend on the width of your windows.

3 Use a miter or handsaw to cut 2 pieces of 1×4 per shutter 2" shorter than the width of each shutter. For example, each of my shutters are the width of 4 pieces of 1×4, with a total width of 14", so I cut my pieces 12" long.

4 Use a palm sander and medium-grit sandpaper to sand each 1×4 piece making sure to remove any splintering wood (see image 1).

5 Use a cotton rag to apply stain to each piece (see image 2). Don't forget the ends and sides. Refer to your can of stain for the recommended dry time before you proceed to the next step.

6 Use a paintbrush to apply 3 coats of polyurethane. Refer to your can of polyurethane for recommended dry time between each coat.

7 After the appropriate dry time, line up the 1×4s that are the same length as your windows side by side and measure 8" down from the top and 8" up from the bottom and mark (see image 3).

8 Run a bead of wood glue on the flat side of 1 of the 12" pieces (or whatever size you made them based on the shutter width you chose) and line up the top of it with the mark at the top of the

shutter and lay it, centered, across the window-length pieces. Use your cordless drill to secure it with 1¼" screws. If you want the screws hidden, screw them in from the back of the window-length pieces into the horizontal 12" piece. They won't be seen when your shutters are open. Just lay the 12" pieces on the ground, then line up the window-length slats on top. Even though you can't see the 12" piece, you can use your tape measure to ensure you attach it in the right spot (see image 4).

9 Run a bead of wood glue on one flat side of another 12" piece and line up the bottom of it with the mark at the bottom of the shutter. Use your cordless drill to secure it with 1¼" screws.

10 Repeat steps 8 and 9 for each additional shutter.

11 Attach your shutter hardware with the screws provided in the packaging at your desired height (see image 5). The exact measurement doesn't matter as long as you attach each shutter using the same measurement so they look uniform once hung.

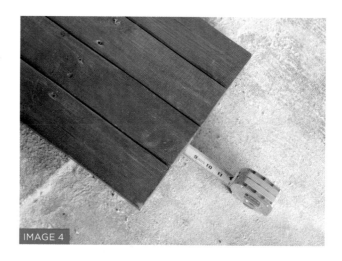
IMAGE 4

IMAGE 5

welcome mat

INVESTMENT: the sanding is the most time-consuming part, but you're still only looking at about an hour of work

SUPPLIES

- 4 pallet slats, 38" long
- 23 pallet slat pieces, 5" long
- medium-grit and fine-grit sandpaper
- 1⅛" screws
- wood stain (optional)
- wood sealer (optional)

TOOLS

- tape measure
- miter or handsaw
- palm sander (optional)
- clamp
- pocket hole jig
- cordless drill
- cotton cloth (optional—for applying stain)
- paintbrush (optional—for applying sealer)

A wood mat would be a fun addition to anything from an outdoor shower to the entrance of a log cabin, where it'd be the perfect spot to leave boots to dry after a day frolicking in the snow. For this specific project, I spent a lot of time sanding my slats smooth. There is always a chance bare feet could find their way onto any mat, so I just wanted to be sure mine was as smooth as possible. My pocket hole jig made this project really easy as well. This isn't exactly an everyday tool, but if you're interested in any kind of woodworking I would seriously consider investing in one. If you don't currently own one, a couple of alternatives for this project could be to use flat brackets screwed into the underside of your mat or even to drill through the thickness of each slat and connect them together with a metal dowel.

For this project I chose a thick slat. These are about 1" thick and I found them all on one heavy-duty pallet. Due to the nature of the project, being an outdoor mat, I figured the thicker the slat, the longer the life she will have.

1 Measure and cut your slats to size using a miter or handsaw. Use your palm sander to sand a flat side of each pallet slat piece thoroughly, first using medium-grit sandpaper and then fine-grit to get a smooth finish (see image 1).

2 Lay out your mat design with the sanded side of your slats facing down. Mark your pocket hole locations on the unsanded side. With full slats 38″ long and pieces cut 5″ long, there will be approximately 6″ between each piece; alternate rows of full slats and rows of pieces with openings (see image 2).

3 One at a time secure the pallet pieces to a work surface and your pocket hole jig with a clamp and drill the pocket holes using your cordless drill. Repeat with the remaining pallet pieces. I decided to drill 2 pocket holes per cut piece to attach them securely into the full slats (see images 3 and 4).

IMAGE 3

the pencil marks show where the pocket holes will go

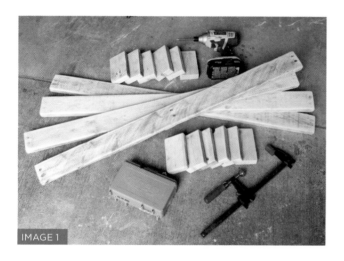

IMAGE 1

IMAGE 2

IMAGE 4

project continued on next page

chapter 5: in the yard   131

4 Connect all of the dots, er, slats through your pocket holes with 1⅛" screws (see image 5). I ended up using 52 screws.

IMAGE 5

each of the pocket holes leads down into the slat below, except for the very bottom slat, for added security I added 4 pocket holes drilled up to attach it to the slat pieces above it

5 If desired, stain and then protect it with a wood sealer (see image 6). This is always optional, but it is a good idea to help extend the life of any project you'll be using outside.

IMAGE 6

wine rack with stemware storage

This project is such a fun addition to any outdoor space. This rustic-chic wine rack with an additional storage rack for stem glassware below is the perfect conversation piece in any eclectic yard. Since it is best to store wine on its side, this piece provides the perfect spot for short-term storage during a backyard gathering or as a serving area for any kind of beverage you're offering. If you don't drink wine, no worries—this same design without the wineglass storage would make a fun magazine rack on a wall or even a cookbook holder for your kitchen.

INVESTMENT: there are some detail cuts that take a little extra time; just consider it the right amount of time to let your white wine chill while you make this totally free project

SUPPLIES

- 1 full pallet with notched support boards
- 2" screws
- 1 wineglass (to use as a measuring guide)
- 2 scrap pallet slat pieces, about 2" wide
- medium-grit sandpaper

TOOLS

- speed square
- reciprocating saw (or circular saw, jigsaw, or miter or handsaw)
- sawhorses (optional, depending on the saw used)
- table saw (optional, depending on pallet slat widths)
- tape measure
- cordless drill
- jigsaw
- palm sander (optional)

1   Lay the full pallet on the ground with the notched side of the support boards facing up (see image 1).

2   Use a speed square to mark a line on each support board of your pallet that lines up with the top of the second slat from the end on the back side of your pallet (see image 2). Depending on the width of your pallet slats and how far apart they are attached to the support boards, you will end up cutting your support boards about 10–12″ long and there will be 1 pallet slat attached to the front and 2 attached to the back.

3   Use your saw to cut each support board on your mark (see image 3). I used a reciprocating saw because I could just prop up that end of the pallet on 2 pieces of 2×4 scrap wood and cut. If you would prefer to set your pallet on a set of sawhorses, you could use a circular saw, jigsaw, or even a handsaw.

4   You might not have this, but my support boards stuck out a little beyond the pallet slats at the end. If yours do the same, cut them flush with the pallet slat with a reciprocating saw (see image 4).

IMAGE 1

I didn't bother to clean the full pallet first since I was only going to be using a small part of it

IMAGE 2

IMAGE 3

IMAGE 4

project continued on next page

5 Measure the depth of your entire pallet (see image 5).

6 Remove a pallet slat of the right width (based on the measurement in step 5) from the pallet you just cut apart. Use your cordless drill to attach it to the bottom of your pallet piece with 2" screws, using 2 per support piece (see image 6). You might need to rip a pallet slat to size with a table saw, but I got lucky and had one just the right width.

IMAGE 5

IMAGE 6

7 You could stop right here and just finish her off with some sanding and maybe a personalized message like "Sean's Reserve Collection," but where there's wine there needs to be wineglasses, so let's add a rack along the bottom for some convenient wineglass storage.

8 Cut off 1 more pallet slat from that same pallet with the same measurement from step 5.

9 Using a wineglass as a guide and a tape measure to ensure equal distance between each glass, mark how far apart you would like each wineglass to hang upside down from the rack (see image 7). As a frame of reference, my wine rack measures 40" long and I decided 5" looked like a good distance apart for the wineglasses.

10 Using the equally spaced marks as a guide, use a speed square to mark U-shaped openings that are about 3" long and 1" wide (see image 8).

11 Use a jigsaw to cut out each U-shaped opening. Did all of my cuts come out exactly the same size and shape? Nope. Does it matter? Nope.

12 Cut the pallet slat scraps about 2" × 4" long. They will function as spacers when you attach the wineglass holder board to leave enough of a gap for the base of your wineglasses.

13 Lay the wine rack on its back. Line up the 2" pieces of pallet slat with each end of the wine rack along the bottom side. Layer the

pallet slat with your U-shaped openings (openings facing the front of the wine rack) on top of the 2″ pallet slat pieces (so the 2″ pieces are creating a gap between the wineglass holder slat and the wine rack). Mark and then drill 2 pilot holes with your ⅛″ drill bit; these hole will go through the wineglass holder slat and the 2″ pallet slat pieces. Make 2 holes per slat piece about 2″ apart (see image 9).

14 Use your palm sander with medium-grit sandpaper to sand every piece of the entire project now, before you attach the wineglass holder board. It will be easier to sand in each of the wineglass holder cuts before assembly.

15 Line up everything as you did in step 13. Use 2 (2″) screws per end to attach the wineglass holder to the scrap pieces and onto the bottom of your wine rack.

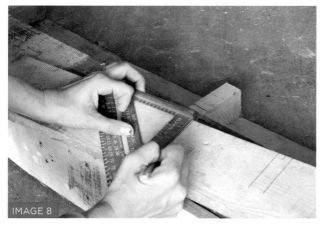

mark where to cut openings to hang your wineglasses; these are about 5″ apart

project continued on next page

16 Just to prove that most projects don't work out as planned, a couple of little pieces of the pallet slat broke off as I was cutting the U shapes (see image 10). Did they not know they were supposed to end up in a book?. But that ended up giving me the perfect opportunity to try something I've wanted to try for a while—using a rake as another eclectic way to hold wineglasses (see image 11). I've actually had this rake on hand for a while; when the handle broke off it I just couldn't get myself to throw it out.

17 To attach the rake to the wine rack, I just found a drill bit slightly larger than the

IMAGE 10

Tip!!!

At thrift stores and yard sales, keep an eye out for rusty old items that you can upcycle into something else entirely, like we did with the rake in this project.

IMAGE 11

rake handle so the handle would fit through it. Drill this hole up through the bottom of the wine rack from one of the cut-outs that had broken. Then I used a small nail wedged in the small opening of the handle of the rake as a makeshift pin to prevent the handle from sliding back out of the hole. (See images 12–14.)

18 To hang the wine rack, I used 2" screws to attach it directly to the wooden fence around our yard; the stability of the fence provides the right amount of support for this piece that can get heavy filled with full bottles of wine.

IMAGE 12

IMAGE 14

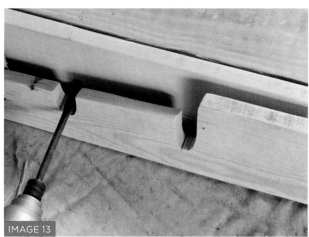
IMAGE 13

planter box
with mitered corners

Now, I'm no green thumb but I figure if my planter boxes are at least cute, people might not notice the near-death experience most of my plants seem to be having. Ahhh, the power of distraction. (A reminder: don't plant anything you are going to eat in a planter made out of pallets. Check out all of the general pallet wood precautions in Chapter 1.)

A pair of these cute little planter boxes would look so great flanking a front door or walkway. Or, place one after another on your porch steps. Using pressure-treated wood if you're buying it new is always a good idea for any project that will live outside—the treatment helps prevent decay and insect infestation. You could even adjust the measurements of this design and make a long, narrow rectangle shape and fill in an otherwise neglected area of your yard with a planter box that will look good whether or not you can keep the flowers in them alive.

For this project, the mitered corners in the tutorial add an extra level of difficulty. If you don't feel like you're quite there yet, use brackets and attach your corners that way. Or maybe this is the project where you decide to tackle that new skill. Go for it! As always, I encourage you to use what pallet wood you have on hand. I've outlined this tutorial specific to the measurements of the pallet slats I had available, so be sure to double-check all your measurements as you go. To begin this project, I used 6 full-length pallet slats measured and cut into 12 equal-length pieces, but your overall measurement for these doesn't have to match this tutorial exactly. So, you've got options, and who doesn't love options?

INVESTMENT: a couple hours, and the cost of an 8'-long 1×4 and a bit of plywood, unless you are using wood pieces you already have

SUPPLIES

- 12 pallet slats, cut 17" long
- 8 (1×4) wood pieces, cut the measurement of the width of 3 slats side by side, mine were 11⅜" long
- medium-grit sandpaper
- paint or stain (optional)
- 1⅛" screws
- 13¾" square piece of ¾" plywood (or whatever scrap wood you have on hand)
- 4 (1×2) wood pieces, 9" long
- wood glue
- 1¼" nails

TOOLS

- tape measure
- miter saw or handsaw
- palm sander (optional)
- paintbrush
- cordless drill
- table saw
- ⅜" drill bit
- hammer or nail gun

IMAGE 1

instead of using the exact measurements for this tutorial, you can lay 6 pallets slats side by side, measure the longest distance on the shortest board (shown in this photo), and use that distance to determine how long your 12 slats should end up

IMAGE 2

the 1×4 boards will run perpendicular to your pallet slats

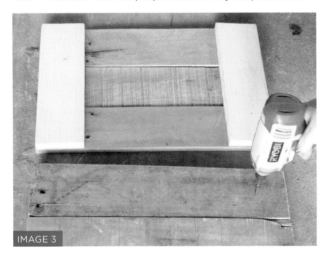

IMAGE 3

1 The planter design has 3 pallet slats running horizontally along each side with 2 1×4s running vertically up each end of each side to create a mitered corner. Use your miter saw to cut the pallet slats and 1×4s according to the measurements provided or to the size of your choice and use your tape measure to find the total height of 3 pallet slats lined up horizontally; then cut the 1×4s to that length (see images 1 and 2).

2 Sand the 1×4s and the pallet slats using a palm sander with medium-grit sandpaper. Paint or stain the 1×4 boards if desired. The paint helps camouflage the difference in the look of the 1×4s and the pallet slats. (And hopefully it will help distract attention from any potential flower misadventures that may end up happening in this very planter).

3 Lay the pallet slats side by side horizontally in 4 separate rows of 3 slats each. Line up the 1×4 boards vertically along the right and left edge of each of the rows, and place them underneath the pallet slats. Use your cordless drill to attach the pallet boards to the vertical pieces with 1⅛″ screws (the sides without the vertical pieces will be the inside of your planter) (see image 3). When attaching your screws stay 2¼″ from the edge to leave room for the miter cut in the next step.

4 Now you have 4 assembled sections that will
be the 4 sides of your planter (see image 4),
and you're ready to miter your corners! Technically,
what we're about to do is called ripping a bevel.
The bevel is the angle you are cutting into the
length of the wood (also known as a beveled edge),
and anytime you cut along the length of a board, as
opposed to chopping a board in half, it is called a
rip cut.

IMAGE 4

5 Adjust your table saw blade to a 45° angle
and double-check to ensure your screws
won't interfere with the blade when you're cutting
(see image 5).

6 Run the 1×4 edges of each side through your
table saw. Make sure the sides with the 1×4
boards attached end up as the longer sides; those
are going to be the outside corners of your planter
box.

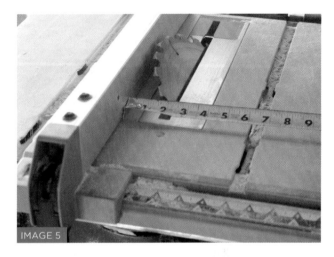

IMAGE 5

7 Measure the width of your pieces from the
back side, inside corner to inside corner (see
image 6).

8 Cut the ¾" plywood (or whatever you have
on hand that would work for the bottom of
your planter) to that measurement. Mine ended up
14" square, but I cut my plywood 13¾" to ensure it
would fit ~~because me and measuring don't always
get along~~. Use a ⅜" drill bit to drill drainage holes in
the bottom piece—I drilled 10 holes.

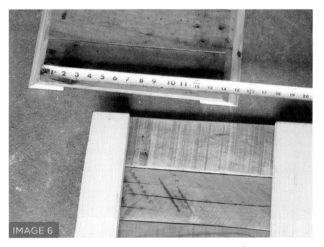

IMAGE 6

project continued on next page

line up the bottom of the 1×2 with the bottom edge of
each planter side

IMAGE 8

IMAGE 9

9 Use a miter or handsaw to cut the 1×2 pieces
to length, about 2" shorter than the size of
your plywood from the previous step will work.
Attach a 1×2 to each planter side, roughly centered
and lined up with the bottom, with 1⅛" screws
(see image 7). These little 1×2 pieces serve two
purposes:

1. they create an easy ledge to support the
   bottom square piece

2. they leave room for drainage in the bottom of
   your planter

10 Run a bead of glue along the mitered corner of a side panel, line that corner up to
the mitered corner of the next side panel, and use
a hammer or nail gun to secure with 1¼" nails (see
images 8 and 9). Repeat this process, connecting
each mitered corner of each side panel to create a
square.

11 Insert the 13¾" square piece into the bottom of the planter to rest on the 1×2s, and
get to planting. A peace lily fills the planter out
nicely, or a fern could be a nice accent to a porch or
patio.

Tip!!!

When attaching mitered corners, it looks nice if you
hammer all the nails into only two of the sides, leaving two
sides without any nail holes. If you think your piece needs
nails from every side, you can always use wood filler in
each nail hole and repaint if you'd like a cleaner look.

cooler surround

There aren't many things more fun than a backyard barbecue with family and friends. Lounging on a warm summer's day, drinking an ice-cold beverage, and shooting the breeze with your favorite people. Add this rustic cooler surround with a built-in bottle opener to the mix and not only does it make your beverages easy to reach, but it also adds a little style to the standard old cooler.

This tutorial assumes a ¾"-thick pallet slat and a Styrofoam cooler measuring 14½" long, 12" wide, and 12" deep. Measure the thickness of your slats and the size of your cooler to determine the exact length of nails and screws that will work best for your project and exactly how many slats you will need to cover your cooler. You will want your pallet slats, when lined up side by side horizontally, to measure at least 3" longer in width than the height of your cooler. Also, 4×4 posts are easy to find at any lumberyard, but I was able to reuse our old patio posts that we updated to a thicker, chunkier option; that's why you'll notice they already have some chippy white paint on them.

INVESTMENT: there are a few little parts that need to be purchased for this project, and overall it will probably take only an afternoon of work

SUPPLIES

- Styrofoam cooler, 14½" × 12" × 12"
- 22 pallet slats, ¾" thick:
  - 10 pallet slats, 12" long (the same length as the width of your cooler)—4 are used for each end of the cooler surround and 2 are used for additional support on each end of the legs
  - 10 pallet slats, 16" long (the same length as your cooler plus 1½")—4 are used for each side of the cooler surround and 2 are used for additional support on each side of the legs
  - 2 pallet slats, 14½" long (the same length as your cooler)—these support the bottom of the cooler
- 1¼" screws

- 4 (4×4) posts, 27" long
- 2" screws
- 4 pallet slats, 12" long (the same length as the width of your cooler—for the lid)
- wood glue
- 2 pallet slats ripped 1¾" wide* with mitered corners on the edge side, 12" long on the short side (for the edge around the lid)
- 2 pallet slats ripped 1¾" wide* with mitered corners on the edge side, 14½" long on the short side (for the edge around the lid)
- 1¼" nails
- all-purpose adhesive
- medium-grit sandpaper
- sink drain screen

- tub and tile adhesive caulk
- drain plug
- bottle opener (the kind that can be screwed onto something)
- 1 handle with hardware

TOOLS

- tape measure
- miter saw or handsaw
- clamp
- pocket hole jig
- cordless drill
- carpenter's square
- table saw
- hammer or nail gun
- palm sander (optional)
- serrated knife

*the 1¾" width is the distance from the top of the already assembled cooler surround to the top of the Styrofoam lid plus the thickness of the pallet slats you are using for the lid; double-check the measurement of your cooler lid and pallet slats before making these cuts

1 Remove any handles from your cooler. (The plastic kind tend to break right off with the just the force of your own strength.)

2 Use a tape measure to measure the size of your cooler (we will worry about the lid a little bit later), length, width, and height. Since we're not mitering the corners, add 1½" to the measurement of the longest side of your cooler, but measure the end at exactly the cooler measurement. For example, my cooler is 14½" long, so I cut the slats for those sides 16" long, and my cooler is 12" wide, so I cut the slats for those sides 12" long.

3 Make all of the pallet slat cuts for the surround with your miter or handsaw.

4 Line up the 4 slats for each side of the surround side by side horizontally with what will end up facing the outside of the cooler surround facing down (see image 1). Mark where to drill your pocket holes, 3 holes per slat should do. Include a few marks at each end to attach each side panel together to create the rectangle shape.

5 Use a clamp to secure each slat to a work surface and your pocket hole jig and drill pocket holes on your marks with your cordless drill.

6 Use a cordless drill and 1¼" screws to attach the slats through the pocket holes (see image 2).

7 Attach the 4 side panels with 1¼" screws, creating an empty rectangle (see image 3).

IMAGE 2

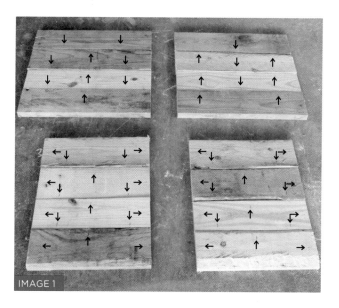

IMAGE 1

IMAGE 3

project continued on next page

IMAGE 4

8   Pray your cooler fits inside—kidding!

9   Put your cooler inside your surround and line up the top of the cooler with the top of the surround. The bottom row of pallet slats will extend below your cooler (see image 4).

10   Flip it over so the top of the cooler is resting on the ground, and let's add our bottom supports.

11   Drill 2 pocket holes in each end of the pallet slats that are cut the same length as the length of your cooler.

12   Using your cordless drill and 1¼" screws, attach the bottom supports inside the bottom of the surround through the pocket holes and into the surround (see image 5).

13   Set the cooler and surround aside and measure and cut the 4×4 posts with your miter saw.

14   Lay the 4×4 posts on the ground in sets of 2 side by side and 12" apart from outside to outside.

15   Lay the 12" leg support slats perpendicular across each pair of 4×4 posts. The bottom of the pallet slat will measure 7" from the bottom of the 4×4 posts, and the end of each slat will line up with the edge of each 4×4 post (see image 6).

16   Use 2" screws, 2 per slat per 4×4, to attach the slats to the 4×4 legs.

IMAGE 5

IMAGE 6

17 Use a carpenter's square lined up with the edge and bottom of the posts to check for square (see image 7).

18 Now rotate the 2 sets of 4×4 posts so the 12" slats that you just attached run vertically up away from the ground. The pairs of legs should be 14½" apart from the outside to outside if each leg and the 12" slat that is attached will be on the outside of each leg.

19 Line up 1 of the 16" leg support slats with the outside edge of the already attached 12" slat and attach with 2" screws, 2 per 4×4 (see image 8).

20 Flip everything over so the 16" slat you just attached is lying on the ground and line up the final 16" slat with the already attached 12" slats, and attach with 2" screws.

21 Stand the legs up and set the cooler surround over the legs. You could attach the surround to the legs here with 2" screws, but I think it is nice to have the parts removable for ease in carrying it and storage.

22 Now, for the lid. This part can be a bit of a challenge depending on the width of the slats you have available. With what I had, it worked best to run the slats for the lid from front to back. Depending on your measurements, you may need to rip a slat so it's the correct width.

23 Measure the length and width at the longest points on the lid that came with your Styrofoam cooler and cut 4 slats the same measurement as the width.

IMAGE 7

IMAGE 8

24 Lay the 4 cut slats side by side and make any necessary cuts with your table saw so the width of the 4 slats together equals the length of your Styrofoam lid.

25 With the 4 slats side by side, and what will be the top of your lid facing down, mark your pocket holes.

project continued on next page

26　Use a clamp to secure each slat to a work surface and your pocket hole jig and drill your pocket holes on your marks with your cordless drill.

27　Run a bead of wood glue between each slat and then attach with 1¼" screws through your pocket holes.

28　With the Styrofoam cooler in the wooden surround, place the Styrofoam lid on the Styrofoam cooler. Lay the attached lid slats on top of the Styrofoam lid and measure the height from the top of the cooler to the top of the lid slats (see image 9).

29　With your table saw, rip your edge pieces to the measurement from the previous step.

30　Use the lid's measurements and miter the corners of the edge pieces on the edge side. Mine were cut 14½" and 12" on the short side of the miter cuts, equal to the measurements of my cooler lid.

31　Lay your lid slats on the ground with your pocket holes visible. Run a bead of glue around each edge and use a hammer or nail gun to attach the mitered edge pieces with 1¼" nails (see image 10).

32　Run beads of all-purpose adhesive on the underside of the lid, where the pocket holes are, and adhere the Styrofoam lid.

33　Now use your palm sander to sand your entire cooler surround and lid with medium-grit sandpaper and read on if you'd like to add a few finishing touches.

34　Time to add a drain. You can find a great selection of sink drain screens and plugs at any big-box home improvement store. Trace around the screen onto the bottom of the cooler and use a serrated knife to cut out the circle. Run a bead of tub and tile adhesive under the lip of the sink screen and insert the screen into the hole so the adhesive seals any gaps to prevent leaking. Insert the drain plug (see images 11–14).

IMAGE 9

IMAGE 10

35 On to the bottle opener! What's a cooler without a way to open the beverages inside? Permanently mounted bottle openers can be found at a variety of online and specialty stores, and they only require a couple of screws to attach. Place yours where you want it and attach.

36 Finally, the handle! For ease of opening, a single handle attached to the center of the top of the lid does the trick. You could also add a couple of hinges to permanently attach the lid to the surround if you'd like. Use the hardware that came with your handle and attach it.

37 Now, who's thirsty?

Tip!!!

Most of the big-box home improvement stores will make cuts for you; it might be easier to transport your 4Ð4 posts home if they are already cut to length at the store.

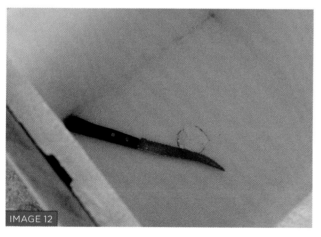
IMAGE 11

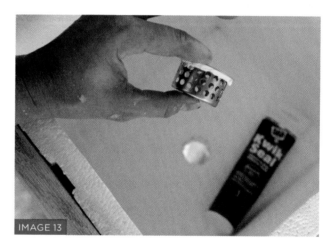
IMAGE 13

IMAGE 12

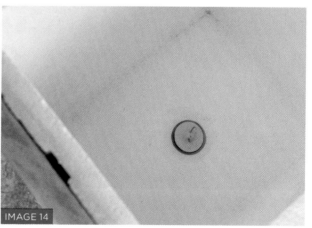
IMAGE 14

chapter 6
furniture

Chunky, rustic wood furniture provides just the right amount of variety throughout your decor, no matter what style. In this chapter, you will find a wide range of furniture pieces—some built from scratch using only wood found on a pallet, to pieces built with a combination of store-bought wood and pallets, to ideas for ways to update your existing furniture to give it that rustic, weathered wood texture. Use these ideas as a starting point for your own projects. Where I've covered our old, wicker nightstand with pallets, maybe your pressed-wood coffee table is the perfect candidate for an upgrade. Or, where I've built a bench maybe you want to make the legs a little taller and turn her into a sofa table. Have at it, and then send me some pictures so I can see your awesome creations.

headboard

This headboard project came about when I discovered the perfect pieces of old beadboard in the most unlikely of spots—the crawl space under our house. The wood was most likely used as some kind of hurricane shutter in a previous life, but don't let what something *used* to be prevent you from transforming it into something new and improved. Here is what she looked like straight out of the crawl space.

Those are just thin strips of a wood beadboard attached horizontally to three thin pieces of wood running vertically up the back; you can see the three rows of nails. (We used the same technique to make the base for the American Flag in Chapter 4.)

This look can easily be replicated with pallet wood instead of beadboard. And you could even run the pallet wood vertically and the boards along the back horizontally. If you need to purchase them, 1×2s or 1×4s would work well for the boards along the back. But you know I'd encourage you to scrounge around for some pallet support boards or other reclaimed wood to use. Why buy when you can find for free?

Hopefully this project helps give you ideas for your very own headboard and ways to use old wood even if you don't end up using pallet wood specifically. Once you start keeping an eye out for reclaimed wood of all kinds, you'll be amazed at where you find it and what you end up using it for.

INVESTMENT: a couple hours and a few dollars if you decide to add the lettering

SUPPLIES

‣ pallet slats, cut to preferred length of headboard
‣ support boards, cut to preferred height of headboard
‣ 1⅛" screws
‣ foam sticker letters (optional)
‣ paint (optional)
‣ medium-grit sandpaper
‣ dark wax (optional)

TOOLS

‣ tape measure
‣ miter or handsaw
‣ cordless drill
‣ paintbrush
‣ palm sander (optional)
‣ natural-fiber brush (optional—to apply the wax)

before

IMAGE 1

IMAGE 2

1   Use a miter or handsaw to cut the pallet slats and support boards to the desired measurements.

2   Lay the pallet slats side by side horizontally over the support boards that are laid vertically and use your cordless drill to attach with screws.

3   To create the "sweet dreams" lettering, simply use foam sticker letters that can be purchased at an arts and crafts supply store for a few dollars (if desired). Use a variety of neutral-colored paints and paint right over the stickers to create a unified yet still uneven and imperfect paint finish. Using a dry-brush paint technique—where there is only a little bit of paint on the very tip of your brush, in a variety of colors—will give you this uneven finish.

4   Remove the foam letters (see image 1), and lightly sand the paint finish with medium-grit sandpaper.

5   Apply a coat of dark wax (see image 2) to further age the look of the paint finish and blend in the very subtle wording detail if desired.

6 If you're looking for more intricate detail or you want a framed headboard, you can easily implement a few of the other techniques we've talked about in other tutorials in this book. For example:

1. for a detailed cut-out design, refer to how we made the Cut-Out Silhouette in Chapter 2 and use that process to transfer a design you like onto your headboard to cut out

2. if you'd like a pallet headboard with a frame around it, you could use a single frame like we do on the Herringbone Coffee Table in Chapter 6 or a double frame similar to the Geometric Wall Art in Chapter 2 and the Barnwood Picture Frame in Chapter 2; if you didn't want to use support boards along the back, you could attach all of the pallet slats within the frame together using pocket holes drilled in the back of them with a pocket hole jig, similar to how we made the Welcome Mat in Chapter 5

3. or, how fun would it be to paint a large American flag on your headboard in a patriotic or vintage-style bedroom? (you can follow the same steps to create the flag image on your headboard that we used in Chapter 4)

7 To hang the headboard, be sure you screw it directly into wall studs to support the weight. Stud finders can be found at most home improvements stores.

large dog bed

Our pups are in the 50–60-pound range and fit nicely in this wonderful bed, but the measurements for the bed can be easily adjusted to suit your dog's size—whether you have an adorable 8-pound puppy or an even larger dog than ours! Perhaps the best part of this project is how easy it is to make. No table saws or pocket holes required. (I will say, for any large piece of furniture, drilling pocket holes so your boards are connected through the center point, creating the maximum strength at each joint, *is* the preferred way to go. But it's up to you. This project will work without them.)

This tutorial assumes you are using at least a ⅝"-thick pallet slat—you may need to adjust the length of the screws you use if your pallet slats are a different thickness.

1 Use your miter or handsaw to cut your pallet slats and 1×2s to size:

1. 4 pallet slats, cut 40" long (for the back)

2. 1 pallet slat, cut 43" long (for the front; I used a wider slat, but you could also use 2 thinner slats)

3. 6 pallet slats, cut 30" long (3 for each side)

4. 2 (1×2) wood pieces, cut 14¼" long (the width of 4 slats laid side by side)

5. 4 (1×2) wood pieces, cut 10¾" long (the width of 3 slats laid side by side)

2 Lay 2 of the 1×2s cut 10¾" on their flat side 30" apart and run beads of glue along them (see image 1).

3 Lay 3 of the pallet slats cut 30" side by side on top of the 1×2s with each end of the pallet slats lined up with the outside edges of the 1×2s (lay the pallets with the side you want facing the outside of the dog bed facing down).

4 Use your cordless drill to attach the pallet slats to the 1×2s with 1¼" screws, 2 per slat at each end (see image 2).

5 Repeat steps 2–4 to assemble the other side and the back. For the back, the side of the pallet slats facing down will end up facing into the dog bed.

6 Use your palm sander to sand each panel with medium-grit sandpaper to remove any splinters.

IMAGE 1

IMAGE 2

project continued on next page

7 Line up each side panel at either end of the back panel and mark on the inside edge of the 1×2 attached to each end of the back panel where to drill 3 pilot holes to attach the back panel to each side panel. Be sure these new holes won't hit any existing screws (see image 3). (If you'd prefer, you could easily just screw each side panel into the back panel, but the first method will minimize the amount of screws you see in your finished project. Feel free to pick your personal preference and go with it.)

8 Drill your pilot holes through your marks with an ⅛" drill bit.

IMAGE 3

mark where to drill pilot holes, making sure they won't hit any existing screws

9 Before lining anything back up, it is easier to get each of your 2" screws started into each pilot hole while the back panel is lying on the ground.

10 Lay 1 side panel on the ground with the 1×2s facing down and line up the edge of the back panel with the edge of that side panel. Attach with the 2" screws through your pilot holes.

11 Attach the other side panel to the back in the same manner.

12 Attach the slat to the front straight through the slat with 2 (1¼") screws at either end. (And for a bit of reality, I cut my front piece 1½" too short—there's just something about me and that tape measure that don't always see eye to eye. But, I didn't have another pallet slat on hand so I used the one I had and only overlapped it on the front by ¾" on each side panel. You won't ever find me claiming that my projects *always* work out perfect on the first try.)

13 Nope, I didn't even add a bottom. I just didn't see the need considering a large pillow was going in there anyway, and more wood would just add to the weight.

14 Now for the real test.

We have a winner. Or is that a treat I'm holding in my hand that she's staring down while waiting patiently for the photo? I will never tell, but you may notice a sliver of a blond ear nice and close, possibly sitting patiently mostly out of camera view waiting for said treat.

Tip!!!

You will have more leverage when you screw in a screw if you have something providing resistance. Laying the side panel on the ground to screw into it will let the ground serve as that resistance.

tabletop

I grabbed this sad little rolling cart off of the side of the road one day (with my husband shaking his head in disbelief after I asked him to pull over to check it out) and knew she would look so much better with a rustic wood top. After a quick inspection to make sure there wasn't anything structurally wrong with her, I brought her home with me. She's on wheels and the locking lever even still works, so it's easy to move around to different spots in our home. She's the right height for a side table or nightstand and would even make a fun bar cart in our dining room or on the back porch when we have friends over for a barbecue. But even if you don't have a rolling cart castaway, this tutorial is designed to help you make a tabletop of any size to suit your own needs.

Here is what the cart looked like to begin with.

This tabletop measures 16″ × 13½″, so the measurements in this tutorial work for that size but this is the perfect project for adding some charm to any old table base or piece of furniture you have that could use some reviving.

1   Remove the old tabletop from the base. Mine was secured with a few screws (see image 1).

2   Take the table base outside and use your palm sander with medium-grit sandpaper to sand the entire base to remove any rust (if you're using a metal table too) and scuff it up for better primer and paint adhesion.

3   Clean the table and wipe it dry to remove any loose dirt, paint, and debris.

IMAGE 1

IMAGE 2

4   Use painter's tape to cover any areas you don't want painted (see image 2).

5   Prime with spray primer. Let dry according to the product directions.

6   Paint the table base. Textured paint helps hide any imperfections in old pieces. You can find textured paint in most stores that sell regular spray paint.

7   With all of the prep work done on the base, it's time to make the new pallet slat tabletop. This same design can be made for any number of bases, so keep your eyes peeled for any cute-legged tables at thrift stores. (Or even on the side of the road—oftentimes people toss out a perfectly good table base because the top of the table has been damaged. Their trash can become your pallet tabletop treasure.)

8   Lay out your pallet slats and use a tape measure and miter or handsaw to cut them to your desired measurements.

9   Cut your 1×2 pieces to be used as trim around the bottom edge of your tabletop. You want 2 the exact width of your tabletop and 2 the length minus 1½″. The reason for cutting the 1×2 pieces equal to the width and 1½″ shorter than the length is to allow for overlap at the corners. If you cut all of these trim pieces the exact dimensions as your tabletop, they won't line up properly with the edge of your tabletop. If this kind of math makes you want to take a break, I totally understand—we're in the same boat.

10 Arrange the 1×2 pieces together in the shape of your rectangle tabletop with each end of the longer pieces butting up to the side of the end pieces, edge-side down, and run a bead of wood glue along the top edge (see image 3).

11 Lay your pallet slats on top of the 1×2s and use a hammer or nail gun to attach with 1¼″ nails, 3 or 4 per slat at each end and every 3–4″ along the side) (see image 4).

IMAGE 3

the shorter pieces are 18″ (the actual width of the finished tabletop) and the longer pieces are 30½″ (the length of the finished tabletop minus 1½″ to account for the overlap at the corners

IMAGE 4

12 Wipe off excess glue with a wet rag.

13 Paint or stain and customize the tabletop if desired.

14 Set your tabletop on your base and use an adjustable wrench to attach from the underside with nuts and bolts for maximum stability. You could also use simple screws if that's easier, depending on the size and shape of your base.

15 Now she's all assembled and ready for a party. I think the juxtaposition of the industrial cart base with the rustic wood top is fun. And who doesn't need a little turquoise in their life? Now picture me wheeling her around from room to room trying to decide where she belongs.

Tip!!!

For two pieces you need to cut exactly the same length, cut them together with your miter or handsaw. Start by cutting a sliver off the ends of newly bought wood to ensure straight ends, then line those ends up and make the cut at your desired measurement. My dad taught me that. Thanks, Dad!

Adirondack-like chair

This chair is the perfect addition to any whimsical outdoor space or rustic living area. Believe it or not, you don't even need to dismantle all of the pallets to make it. When you're picking up pallets for this project, look for ones that don't have wide gaps between the slats. If need be, you can also attach additional slats between any extra-wide gaps once you get them home (see image 1). We wouldn't want anyone falling through their chair.

Take extra care when sanding since you'll be sitting in and lounging on her when she's done. You might not find the wood alone the most comfortable spot to sit, but that's nothing a nice thick cushion can't remedy. Be sure to buy pillows made to stand up to the elements if you plan to leave them outside. The measurements in this tutorial are specific to the measurements of the full pallets used; double-check your measurements as you go. If you want a frame of reference, measure to see how high your sofa is to determine a good height for this seat.

IMAGE 1

INVESTMENT: this project only takes a couple of hours and doesn't really cost a thing if you're using all pallet wood

SUPPLIES

- 2 full pallets about 30" square (1 for the chair seat and 1 for the chair back)
- 4 pallet support boards about 12" long (you can use 2×4s if you don't have any support boards on hand)
- 2" screws
- ⅛" drill bit (optional)
- 4 pallet support boards about 24" long (for the legs)
- 4" screws
- 3 support boards about 35½" (for the arms and back support)
- 3" screws
- multiple grits of sandpaper, ranging from course to fine

TOOLS

- tape measure
- reciprocating saw (if you need to cut a pallet to size)
- miter or handsaw
- hammer or mallet
- cordless drill
- carpenter's square
- palm sander (optional)

IMAGE 2

IMAGE 3

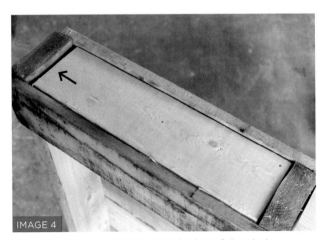

IMAGE 4

this gap will end up hidden by the leg of the chair

1 If necessary, measure and cut your full pallets to your desired size with your reciprocating saw. The pallet for my seat measures 29″ square. I cut a 32″ square pallet down to 29″ wide so it would line up with the width of the seat (see image 2), but left the height at 32″.

2 Use a miter or handsaw to cut the 4 support boards 12″. Insert them into the open sides of the pallet slat you will use for the seat, 2 per side (the sides are the edges of the pallet that do not have support boards running along them). You may need to use a hammer or mallet to help them into place (see image 3).

3 These supports don't have to fit perfectly. These sides of the pallet will be the sides of the chair (not the front and back), so if they are a little too short, make them touch the middle support board that is in the pallet and runs perpendicular to where you are inserting the support board pieces. Any gap at either end will end up hidden behind the legs (see image 4).

4 Use your cordless drill and 2″ screws to attach these new support pieces. Drill through the pallet slats and into each new piece, 2 screws per piece from both the top and the bottom of the pallet. You can drill pilot holes with an ⅛″ drill bit if you want to prevent the pallet slats from splitting, but it's not required.

5 Use a miter or handsaw to cut the 4 pallet support boards for the legs 24″ long.

6　Use your tape measure to measure and mark 15″ up the inside of 2 of your leg support boards.

7　Lay those 2 legs on the ground about 30″ apart with the marks facing each other and line up the top of the pallet for the seat with your marks. Line up each side of the pallet with the inside edge of each leg, then check for square with your carpenter's square (see image 5).

IMAGE 5

8　Using your cordless drill and 4″ screws, attach the legs to the side of the pallet. Drill from under the pallet, through the pieces you attached in step 4 and into your leg boards (see image 6).

9　Repeat steps 6–8 to attach the other 2 legs to the opposite side of the pallet. You now have a backless seat (see image 7).

10　Measure the width of your seat, from the outside of 1 leg to the outside of the other leg; mine measured 35½″.

IMAGE 6

11　Cut 1 pallet support board for the back support to this measurement with a miter or handsaw.

12　Line up this support board horizontally along the back of the 2 back legs. Line up the top edge of the support board with the top of the legs. The flat side of the support board should be facing into the seat. Attach through the support board into the legs with 2 or 3 (3″) screws at each end (see image 8).

IMAGE 7

project continued on next page

chapter 6: furniture　　169

13 Measure from the back of the just attached support board to the front of the front legs and add about 5″ to that length (if you are following the measurements provided, it should be about 35½″).

14 Cut the last 2 support boards to that length with a miter or handsaw—they will become the arms of the chair.

IMAGE 8

IMAGE 9

15 Line up each of these support boards on either side of the seat, with one end lining up with the back of the support board that runs horizontally across the back and the flat side of the board facing down; they will overhang the legs in the front (see image 9).

16 Attach with 3″ screws, 2 or 3 screws into each leg.

17 Sand the entire project, including the pallet for the back (which isn't attached yet). Start with course-grit sandpaper and then use medium grit, maybe even finishing with fine-grit sandpaper on the arms.

18 Rest the pallet for the back at whatever angle you desire up against the support board running across the back. It is not necessary to attach it, and it is nice to have the flexibility to adjust the angle depending on how "loungy" you're feeling on any given day.

19 Add cushions and pillows as desired.

bench with decorative angle cuts

A bench is a great alternative to traditional chairs and can be used in any space. You could adjust these dimensions and make a really long bench, or even make the legs longer and turn it into a sofa table, or make the legs longer *and* wider apart and you could make yourself a whole table, with matching benches. For as beautiful as this turned out, the process is surprisingly straightforward. The use of the table saw to make all of the rip cuts (cutting a board along the length of it to make it narrower) isn't absolutely necessary; feel free to leave any of those pieces full-width if you don't have access to a table saw. The idea of making a bench intimidated me at first, so I decided to make a design without a back. Having a back to lean on while you're sitting on your bench would be a nice feature, but this is a good project to get started with furniture making—and you never know, maybe we'll include a bench with a back in the next book.

Since this is a project intended for regular use and requires stability, I highly recommend using a pocket hole jig and drilling pocket holes at the connections, but L brackets are always an alternative. And, um, I had to look up what each bench piece was called so I could easily describe it for you instead of referring to it as "the piece that's kind of floating in the middle and helps secure the legs in place." A quick "furniture-making terminology" Internet search helped me sound smarter than I probably am.

INVESTMENT: this project is made completely of pallet wood and only took a few hours to complete; I'm willing to bet that whatever time you lose in the process will be more than made up for in the amount of happiness you will feel about your new bench

SUPPLIES
- 7 pallet slats at least 60" long
- 1¼" screws
- 1½" screws
- 1¼" nails
- medium- and fine-grit sandpaper
- wood glue
- 2" nails

TOOLS
- tape measure
- miter or handsaw
- table saw
- clamp
- pocket hole jig
- cordless drill
- hammer or nail gun
- palm sander (optional)

1 Use your tape measure and miter or handsaw to measure and make these cuts in your pallet slats, and use your table saw to make the rip cuts.

1. 4 pallet slats cut 40" long (for the top)

2. 4 pallet slats cut 16½" long (for the legs)

3. 4 pallet slats cut 13" long and ripped in half (for the legs)

4. 2 pallet slats cut 11" long (for the side apron)

5. 2 pallet slats cut 11" long and ripped in half (for side stretchers)

6. 2 pallet slats cut 32" long (for the apron)

7. 1 pallet slat cut 30½" long and ripped in half (for the stretcher—double-check your measurements; this is based on pallet slats ¾" thick)

8. 2 pallet slats at least 19" long and ripped in half (for the decorative angled cuts)

2 For each leg, you will need: 2 pieces 16½" long; 2 pieces 13" long, ripped in half; 1 piece 11" long, called the side apron; and 1 piece 11" long, ripped in half, called the side stretcher (see image 1).

3 Using image 2 as a guide, mark where to drill your pocket holes and then use your clamp to secure each wood piece to your pocket hole jig and a work surface and drill your pocket holes with your cordless drill. You want 3 along one side of each 13"-long piece and 2 in each end of both the side apron and the side stretcher (see image 2).

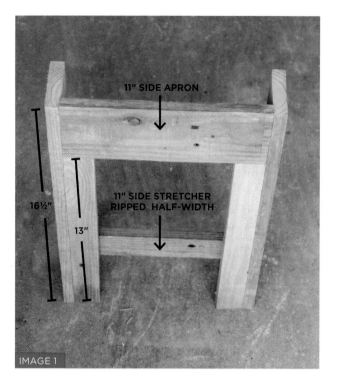

IMAGE 1

IMAGE 2

project continued on next page

IMAGE 3

IMAGE 4

4 Lay both 13"-long pieces vertically, pocket holes facing up, 11" apart from outside edge to outside edge. Lay the side apron, pocket holes facing up, perpendicular to the 13"-long pieces and along the top of them, so each end of the side apron lines up with the outside edges of the 13"-long pieces and is right above them.

5 With the edge side facing down, line up each 16½" long piece with the pieces lying flat and attach them through the pocket holes using 1¼" screws. The bottom of the 16½" long piece will line up with the bottom of the 13" long piece, creating the bottom of the leg, and the top will line up with the top of the side apron.

6 Use your tape measure to measure 4" up from the bottom. Line up the bottom of your side stretcher with that mark and attach the side stretcher to the legs through the pocket holes with 1¼" screws (see image 3).

7 Repeat steps 2–6 to make the other leg.

8 Drill 2 pocket holes in each end of both side apron pieces. Be sure the new holes will clear any screws already in place.

9 Use 1¼" screws to attach each side apron with the top edge lined up with the top of each leg.

10 Center the 30½"-long piece (the stretcher) between the side stretchers and attach with 2 (1½") screws through each end (see image 4).

11 Use a miter saw to cut both 19"-long decorative pieces at a 35° angle at one end on the flat side and at a 55° angle on the flat side at the other end. The slat will end up 19" long on the long edge and 15⅝" long on the short edge (see image 5). The decorative angled cuts are optional so feel free to leave them out if you prefer.

12 Attach the angle pieces (with the longer edge facing up) with a few 1¼" nails in each end; the 35° cut attaches to the center of the side apron and the 55° cut attaches to the top of the stretcher where the 2 decorative pieces meet in the middle.

13 Sand everything—including the 4 boards for the top of the bench that are not yet attached—with a medium-grit sandpaper and then a fine-grit for a very smooth finish.

14 Paint or stain if desired. This bench has a finish of Annie Sloan Chalk Paint in Old White on everything but the seat. The stain on the seat is ZAR brand in the color Modern Walnut. If you want to hide the pocket holes, you could fill them with wood filler before you paint.

15 Center the boards for the seat across the top of the assembled legs and aprons, and use your tape measure to check for an equal overhang on each end and side. Glue and attach with 2" nails, 3 per board per end (see image 6).

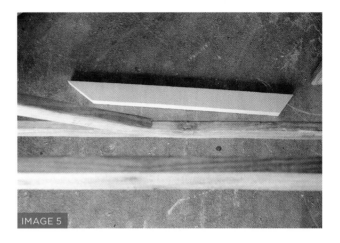

IMAGE 5

IMAGE 6

Tip!!!

If you don't have a table saw to rip your pallet slats in half, you can always buy 1×2s for those pieces of wood. If your pallet slats are ¾" thick, they will be the same thickness as a 1×2.

herringbone coffee table

This is one of those projects best made with pallet slats of the same thickness for a nice, even tabletop. With that said, I did not follow that advice and I still love the look and the little imperfections. (We just need to be extra careful with our wineglasses.) Another idea would be to make this pattern and attach the frame around the edges with a ¼" lip and have a piece of ¼"-thick glass cut to fit. That way you could lay the glass over the design to create a smooth surface and still enjoy the design underneath.

Don't be intimidated by the design of this table. I would file this project in the "not hard, but time-consuming" category. Get your sawing hands ready and settle in; I think this one is definitely worth the effort. I know it looks like a lot of intricate cuts, but don't let any fear of getting things perfect stop you from attempting this coffee table. Were all of my cuts perfect so each piece fit together like a designer puzzle? Nope. The unique way it all went together just adds to the one-of-a-kind feel, says the girl whose coffee table has a few gaps here and there. It just goes to prove that it doesn't have to be perfect to be something you love.

If you don't have a miter saw, you might seriously consider buying one now, with the final project including about 150 different pieces of wood. Making those cuts with a handsaw would prove to be quite the arm workout, but with a miter saw you could bust them all out and have this project complete in about a day.

Adjust my measurements as needed to fit your space. You can even make the small pieces for your herringbone pattern a larger scale if you prefer. If you decide to make a larger coffee table, you might want to consider adding a third rectangular leg underneath the middle to prevent sagging over time. You can also paint, stain, or varnish this piece for a more finished look, but I'm loving the simplicity of the bare wood, so this one is staying as is. For now.

INVESTMENT: it will take about a day to make this table, but the legs and the plywood base are the only purchases required

SUPPLIES

- 10 pallet slats at least 2⅝" wide, all of the same thickness ~~ideally~~
- 1 piece ½"-thick MDF, cut 36" × 24" (you could have it cut for you at most home improvement stores)
- wood glue
- 8 pieces 1½" × 1½" poplar (for the table legs):
  - 4 pieces 17½" long
  - 4 pieces 21" long
- 2½" screws
- 1½" screws
- 2 pallet slats (for the table edge)
- 1¼" nails
- medium- and fine-grit sandpaper

TOOLS

- tape measure
- table saw
- miter saw
- palm sander (optional)
- carpenter's square
- clamp
- pocket hole jig
- cordless drill
- 1 small- and 1 medium-size drill bit; one bit needs to be slightly larger than the head of your screws, the other bit should be slightly smaller than the threads of your screws
- hammer or nail gun

1 Cut all of the pieces for your herringbone pattern from the 10 pallet slats. Mine are 5″ × 1¼″, and you'll need about 150 pieces. The majority of the slats I used for this project were 2⅝″ wide, so 2 (1¼″) strips could be ripped on the table saw out of each slat, then those strips were cut into 5″ lengths with the miter saw.

2 Lay out your herringbone pattern on the ground, otherwise known as a chevron or zig-zag pattern. Create the pattern with the rectangular pieces overlapping at each end and "zigzagging" back and forth to create 90° angles. Some edges might need to be sanded down here so each piece fits together snugly (see image 1). This "dry fitting" step will let you see how it all fits together. Some pieces might work better next to each other, and some cuts could have been just a little off. Adjust as necessary at this stage.

3 Use small scrap pieces to fill in around the edges and complete the design forming a rectangle (see image 2).

4 Run a bead of wood glue along the back of each 5″ × 1¼″ piece and attach your design, as you've laid it out, onto your piece of MDF. As long as your MDF base is cut at a right angle (if you're making your coffee table round or oval, you will want to start by drawing guide lines directly onto your MDF to follow and keep you herringbone pattern running straight), line up the first row of your herringbone pattern so it is even with one side and one end and continue from there (see images 3 and 4).

IMAGE 1

IMAGE 2

5   Let it dry overnight.

6   Using your miter saw, cut your leg pieces to size: cut 4 pieces 17½" long and 4 pieces 21" long (see image 5).

7   One at a time secure each poplar wood piece that is 21" long to your pocket hole jig and a work surface and drill 2 pocket holes at each end (see image 6).

IMAGE 5

these legs are 1½" × 1½" pieces of poplar, which has a similar look to the color of the pallet wood; they can be found in many home improvement centers near the lattice (you could also use pine boards instead)

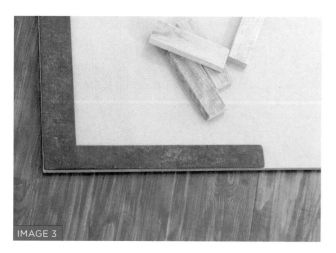
IMAGE 3

IMAGE 4

IMAGE 6

project continued on next page

8 Create 2 rectangles with your 8 pieces of poplar wood with the pocket holes you just drilled facing out from the rectangle. Use wood glue at each connection and 2½" screws in each pocket hole to secure the rectangle together (see images 7 and 8).

9 Drill 3 pilot holes through one of the 21" long pieces in each rectangle, starting from the opposite side of the wood as the pocket holes. This piece will be the top of your rectangle-shaped leg and will get secured into the base of your coffee table. To countersink your screws, first drill ¾" deep with a bit that is slightly larger than the head of your screw and then finish the hole with a bit that is slightly smaller than the threads of your screws. For any hole you drill that you don't want to go all of the way through the wood, use a piece of painter's tape wrapped around the drill bit to indicate when to stop drilling (see images 9 and 10).

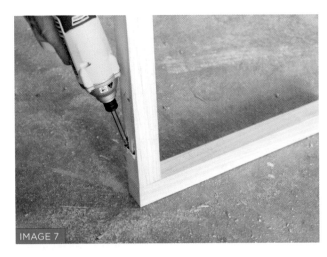
IMAGE 7

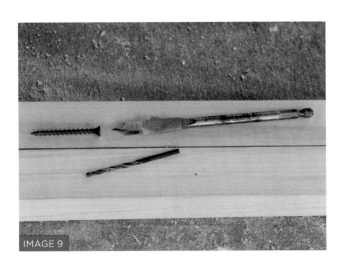
IMAGE 9

IMAGE 8

pocket holes are facing out of the rectangle

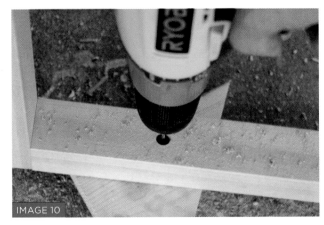
IMAGE 10

prop the piece you're drilling into on a piece of scrap wood to prevent dulling your bit by drilling into the concrete if you happen to be working on your patio, too.

10 Run a bead of glue along the underside of each end of your MDF where you will be attaching the legs and secure each leg to the coffee table with 1½" screws, through your pilot holes and into the MDF (see image 11).

11 Now we'll attach a few pieces that will create a framed look and a smooth edge to hide the MDF from view. If you want to add a glass top to your coffee table, here is where you would attach the frame so it rises above the top of your herringbone pattern the same thickness as the glass you would like to add.

12 Use your tape measure to measure the height from the bottom of the MDF base to the top of the slats in your herringbone pattern on top and run your 2 pallet slats for the edge through the table saw and rip them down to that measurement.

13 Miter the corners at 45° on the edge side, making sure the measurement on the shorter side equals the size of your coffee table; mine is 24" × 36".

14 Attach the frame to the edge of the coffee table with wood glue and then use a hammer or nail gun to secure with 1¼" nails (see image 12).

15 Use a palm sander to sand everything smooth. Start with medium-grit sandpaper and follow with a fine-grit sandpaper.

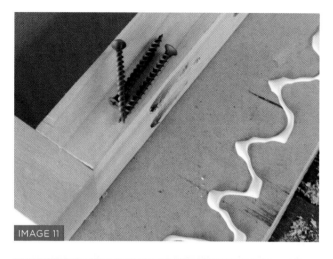
IMAGE 11

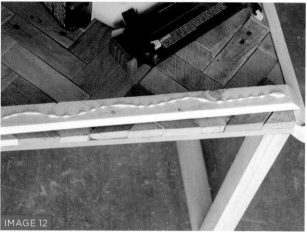
IMAGE 12

Tip!!!

This is a great project for cracked or broken slats. Since you will be cutting the slats into a number of small pieces, many sections of a cracked slat will be usable and the other sections can easily be cut around.

U-shaped side table

I'm going to confess that this project challenged my brain. Sometimes it is easy to overcomplicate a process by trying to anticipate how it will all end up instead of just taking it as it comes. With that said, you can choose to follow this tutorial exactly, with the same measurements, but you may also choose to determine the length of your cuts based on the specific pallet slats you have available. For example, if you have a bunch of 40″ pallet slats lying around, you may want to make your table base 20″ high so you can get two usable pallet slat pieces out of each full slat. I was able to use the scrap left over from the cuts I made for the outside of each side to line the inside of each side because the slats where originally 42″ long. The cuts for the outside were 22″ long, so the pieces left over were 20″ long—not quite long enough to reach the top but long enough to be hidden underneath. Trying to think ahead with these kinds of measurements may ~~give you a headache~~ help you minimize the amount of scrap wood you have left over in the end, but it is definitely not a project requirement. Feel free to just cut as you go and see where it takes you.

I guess this is my way of saying that even though my side table is already at the pretty-picture stage doesn't mean I thought this project was simple. But you can do it; wonky pallet slats can't stop us.

And, as I like to do, I used pallet support boards for the base of my side table because I had them on hand, and I'd always rather use free wood than purchase something new, even if it proves harder to work with. You could also use 2×4s purchased new if you prefer. With this tutorial the specific length of the screw you use will depend on the thickness of the wood you use; just be sure to double-check your measurements as you go.

INVESTMENT: this project gave me more of a test than I was expecting, but over the course of a week and after not having to buy any supplies I felt like I came out on top

SUPPLIES

‣ pallet support boards to create the shape of your side table:
  • 4 boards cut 22″ long
  • 4 boards cut 10½″ long
  • 2 boards cut 17½″ long
  • 2 boards cut 14″ long
‣ 1½″ screws
‣ pallet slats:
  • 10 slats cut 22″ long (for the outside of each side)
  • 5 slats cut 23″ long (for the top)
  • 3 slats at least 24″ long (will be cut to exact size to finish off the front of the side table)
‣ 1¼″ nails
‣ wood glue
‣ 4 additional pallet support boards (optional—to line the underside of your table if desired)
‣ 2″ nails
‣ 10 additional pallet slats (optional—to line the underside of your table if desired)

TOOLS

‣ tape measure
‣ miter or handsaw
‣ pocket hole jig
‣ clamp
‣ cordless drill
‣ hammer or nail gun

1 Measure and cut your support pieces to size with a miter or handsaw and lay out the shape of each side and the top. Mark your pocket holes (see images 1 and 2).

2 Use a cordless drill to drill your pocket holes with your pocket hole jig; use a clamp to secure the jig and wood in place on a work surface (see image 3).

3 Attach the 4 support pieces with 1½" screws through your pocket holes to create the shape of each side and the top (see image 4).

IMAGE 1

one side of the table; some pallet slats come with the support boards notched out—I used that type for this project, but it is not necessary

IMAGE 2

the top of the side table

IMAGE 3

IMAGE 4

4   Drill 3 pocket holes in each side of the top piece—this is where you will connect the top to each side (see image 5).

5   Attach the top to each side through the pocket holes with 1½″ screws (see image 6).

6   Flip your U-shape upside down and you are done with the base of your side table (see image 7).

7   Measure and cut your pallet slats with a miter or handsaw. Using the measurements for this tutorial you will need 10 pieces 22″ long (5 for each side) and 5 pieces 23″ long (for the top).

IMAGE 5

IMAGE 6

IMAGE 7

project continued on next page

8 Attach the pallet slats vertically up each side with 1¼" nails; line up the first slat with the front and top of the attached U-shaped base (see image 8).

9 Glue and clamp any slats that need extra help lying flat, then let dry overnight (see image 9).

10 Attach slats along the top, using 2 or 3 nails per slat at each end (see image 10).

11 Measure along the top of the front of your side table. Cut 1 slat (of the 3 that are at least 24" long) to that length and attach with 1¼" nails, 2 or 3 per end and a few along the top (see image 11).

IMAGE 8

IMAGE 10

I ran out of pallet slats of the same width so I ended up having to use my table saw to rip the back slat along the top to the correct width to line up with the size of the table

IMAGE 9

IMAGE 11

12 Measure from the bottom of the piece you just attached to the ground (on each side just to be sure) and cut the remaining 2 slats to that measurement; line it up with the outer edge of the slat running up the side and attach it with 1¼" nails (see images 12 and 13).

13 You could definitely call it done here—I actually kind of like the quatrefoil-ish detail the notched-out support boards give the look of the inside of each table leg (see image 14). So feel free to skip ahead to your finishing touches like sanding, painting, etc. Or, if you'd like a more finished look, let's keep going.

IMAGE 12

IMAGE 13

IMAGE 14

project continued on next page

IMAGE 15

IMAGE 16

14 Measure the width of each side, from the front to the back of the table (see image 15), and use a miter or handsaw to cut 4 support boards to that length. Use scraps if you can—mine were about 1″ short, but they will end up covered anyway.

15 Attach 1 of the newly cut support boards horizontally along the bottom of the inside and 1 horizontally along the top of the inside of each side with 2″ nails (see image 16).

16 Measure the height from the ground up the inside of each table leg to the bottom of the top piece.

17 Use a miter or handsaw to cut the 10 additional pallet slats to that measurement.

18 Attach the pallet slats vertically up the inside of each side with 1¼″ nails (see image 17).

19 Paint, sand, stain, and/or seal if desired (see image 18).

IMAGE 17

IMAGE 18

night stand with arrow detail

INVESTMENT: a little creative thinking and a few afternoons; cutting all of the little pieces for the arrow detail is the most time-consuming part, but this project doesn't have to cost a penny

SUPPLIES

- 1 square/rectangle piece of furniture
- pallet slats (12 or more depending on the size of your piece)
- 1½" nails
- wood glue
- ¼"-thick plywood (optional—if you need to create any flat surfaces)
- fine-grit sandpaper

TOOLS

- straightedge (optional—if necessary to prepare the furniture piece)
- jigsaw (optional—if necessary to prepare the furniture piece)
- tape measure
- miter saw
- hammer or nail gun
- table saw
- clamps
- palm sander (optional)

I have to admit that I debated even putting a project like this in the book because, really, what are the chances that you have the exact same nightstand that I do? But, even though you might not be working with a dark wicker, three-drawer nightstand, the concepts in this project can be used to update many different kinds of furniture pieces. And as with any upgrade like this where you're essentially lining something with pallet slats, use pallet slats that are all the same thickness if you can to give your finished piece a smooth finish.

Since we're not building a piece of furniture from scratch, if you don't have an item on hand you want to update, IKEA is a home goods store that sells really basic, square-shaped items that would work great for this project. The nightstand I'm updating was something I bought on the cheap in Curaçao and although it is functional, it just isn't our style anymore. She seemed like the perfect candidate for this type of an upgrade, however. I wouldn't suggest pulling out your heirloom pieces here. That thrifted item over there in the corner you've tried to camouflage with accessories will work just perfectly.

A few things to look for that would make an item a good—or bad—choice for this project:

1. a boxy, square shape—the easier to face with pallets
2. flat surfaces—even if an item has a round top, as long as it is flat, you're good to go
3. not a piece you think you'll ever wish you had back—once you go pallet slat you never go back, or however that saying goes

Here is what my nightstand looked like when we started.

1 Clean your furniture piece thoroughly.

2 Remove any existing hardware. If your hardware screws in from the inside of the drawers, you will need to get longer screws or switch out the hardware all together, since we will be adding more depth to each drawer with the addition of the pallet slats.

3 Make any adjustments to your piece to make it as boxy of a shape as possible. I used a jigsaw and cut off the lip where the top of the nightstand overlapped over each side and cut off the legs (see images 1 and 2).

IMAGE 1

IMAGE 2

4 Use your tape measure to measure the height and width of each side of your piece and cut pallet slats to size with a handsaw or miter saw to cover each side without any overlap.

5 Lining up the first slat with the front and the top of your piece, use a hammer or nail gun to attach each slat vertically with 3 (1½″) nails at the top and bottom of each slat. Use wood glue for extra support if desired. Repeat on the other side of your piece until both sides are completely lined (see image 3). You may need to rip the last slat down with a table saw to get it lined up with the back of your piece—or you could just leave it; what's a ½″ or so of empty space between your nightstand and your wall? And since I'm not in the habit of taking my furniture pieces away from the wall just to check them out from the back side, I didn't even line the back of my nightstand with slats, but go for it if you'd prefer.

6 Measure the width of the top, including the additional width created when you added the slats to each side (see image 4). Cut pallet slats to that measurement, enough to fully line the top with slats.

IMAGE 3

project continued on next page

7   Lining up the first slat with the front of your piece, attach each slat to the top with 1½" nails. Make any cuts necessary on the last slat to make it line up with the back of the slats on each side (see image 5).

8   Now for the tricky, er, fun part—the front. It works well to measure each exposed part of your original furniture piece one piece at a time, cut and attach that piece, and move on to measure, cut, and attach the next piece (see images 6, 7, and 8).

IMAGE 6

front before any pallet slats

IMAGE 4

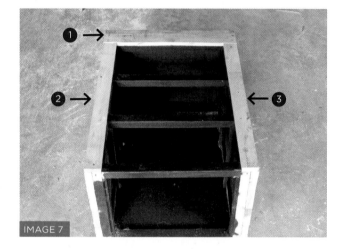

IMAGE 7

IMAGE 5

IMAGE 8

9 Repeat step 8 for as many pieces of pallet slat you need to completely cover your original piece of furniture.

10 For the drawers, you could very easily follow the same method you did for the top and measure the width of each drawer, cut slats to fit, and attach them horizontally across the face of each drawer. There's no harm in the simplicity of that at all.

11 But, in an effort to give this piece a little extra flair all its own, I thought a fun arrow detail on each drawer would kick up the character level just the right amount. I had the thin strips of scrap pallet slats left over from the rip cuts I made to make all of the pieces fit on the front, so here is what I ended up with (see image 9).

12 Let's talk about how to achieve this arrow look. You could definitely incorporate it into other pieces of furniture if you're not working with a nightstand. Make sure you are working with a flat surface. I had to glue a piece of ¼"-thick plywood into the wicker inset of each drawer to create a flat surface to work with (see image 10). If your piece is already flat, you won't need to do this.

13 To create a framed edge for each drawer, rip 4 pieces of pallet slat down to ½" width with mitered corners. You want the measurements of the long sides to equal the width and length of your drawer (see image 11).

IMAGE 10

IMAGE 9

IMAGE 11

project continued on next page

chapter 6: furniture   193

14 Attach the mitered frame pieces to the face of your drawer, lined up with the outer edge of each drawer, with 1¼" nails. Or, if you would like to avoid nail holes, you can glue and clamp each piece and let them dry overnight.

15 For the arrow design, you'll need 12–14 equal-size pieces per drawer. These pieces are the same length on both sides and the same length at both ends, and both ends are cut at a 45° miter cut in the same direction. The miter cut is cut on the flat side of the wood (see image 12).

16 To determine what size you will need each piece to be to fit your drawer face, cut 2 small pieces of pallet slats about ¾" wide (the width of each of these pieces doesn't have to be exact) with mitered corners at one end. Line up the mitered corners so the 2 pieces form the point of the arrow and set them on the drawer to mark where to cut the mitered corner at the other end.

17 Cut along your mark and use those 2 pieces as a template for cutting each additional piece (see image 13).

18 Continue cutting pieces this size to fill your drawer front. Each piece does not have to have the exact same width, but the 2 pieces in each "row" that meet in middle to create the arrow look do need to be the same width for the arrow image to line up correctly (see image 14).

IMAGE 13

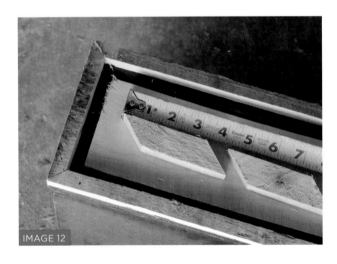
IMAGE 12

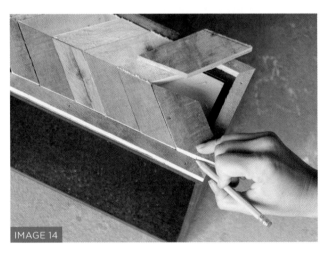
IMAGE 14

19 Mark and cut the small pieces to fill in the corners where full pieces won't fit.

20 Dry fit each drawer face completely with the pieces. Sometimes it's just nice to make sure everything fits together well without the pressure of permanency.

21 Remove all of the pieces, run a bead of glue along the face of your drawer, inside the frame, enough to secure each of your arrow pieces,

and replace the arrow pieces exactly how you had dry fit them on top of the glue (see image 15).

22 Clamp or place a heavy object on each drawer face and let the glue dry overnight.

23 Sand the entire piece thoroughly with a fine-grit sandpaper (see image 16).

24 Replace the drawer hardware and add any finishing details you would like. I chose to mix white paint with water, about 50-50, and just give it a light whitewash. This technique allows the wood detail to show through and just mutes down some of the natural wood tones (see image 17).

IMAGE 15

IMAGE 16

the top drawer hasn't been sanded yet; the bottom drawer has

Tip!!!

For this, and any project where you are lining up slats side by side, sanding down the edges of your pallet slats to remove any splintery wood pieces or rough edges will help the slats line up closer together.

IMAGE 17

chapter 7

the finishing touches

Now for a few fun details to make the beautiful and unique art, craft, and furniture pieces you've made 100 percent custom to you and your home, or as a gift for someone you adore. Here are a few ideas I love. Use these basic instructions to take any of the projects in this book in your own unique direction.

aging new wood

Sometimes you just don't have any reclaimed wood to use or you don't have pieces the right size, and you need to buy new wood for your project. Here are some tools and techniques you can use to make new wood look old.

distressing with tools and equipment

The following items will help you dent, ding, rough-up, scratch, and all-around pepper your wood with marks and give it some "age":

▸ both the head and the claw of a hammer at a variety of angles (see image 1)
▸ hammer in marks from the threads of a screw (see image 2)
▸ wood planer—these scratches are perfect for paint and stain to sink into (see image 3)
▸ a few whacks of a chain, paint can opener, or screwdriver could also do the trick, and hammering any of these items into the wood will create even deeper grooves

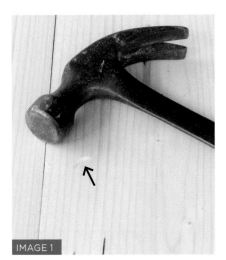

IMAGE 1

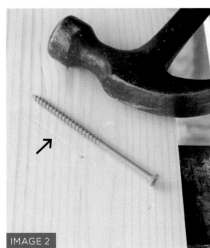

IMAGE 2

IMAGE 3

staining and waxing

After you take your tools to your new wood to create dips and dents, give it a once-over with some stain or wax. These two options can give you a huge range of finishing looks. Don't use wax on projects that will end up outside with direct exposure to sunlight since wax will melt in the heat.

The combination of a dark stain, like a walnut color, with a gray stain, often called driftwood, gives wood a nice weathered look. The more inconsistently you apply it, the more authentically aged it will look. Make sure to get in all of your new grooves and cover up any of that "new wood" look.

notice how all of the dips and dents added to the wood really stand out with a coat of dark stain

painting

Whether you want to paint over stain or just paint an untreated project, you have a number of options:

Ask at your home improvement store if they have any mistinted paint on hand—they will often sell it to you at a deep discount.

- You can layer your paint over the stain to create a deeper "I've lived through many different generations of paint choices" look. For this look use 3–5 different colors with one particularly bright color and one white. Apply a little bit of each color, in an inconsistent application, using a dry-brush technique (with just a little bit of paint right on the tip of your brush, creating an uneven paint finish) so the paint application is somewhat streaky.

- At any point while painting, you can take a scraper and remove some of the paint in between coats. This will give it a chipped look and is easiest to accomplish when the paint is barely dry, since it is easier to remove.

- If you're running low on paint, you can always use a little water to help it spread farther. Since we're going for a rustic, distressed look in the end anyway, any imperfections in the coverage will just add to the character.

the very bottom board contains layers of paint and the board above it has been scraped to show layers underneath

sanding

Sanding can accomplish many things, from creating a super-smooth finish to melding together all the steps above in an aged look and revealing a bit of each layer of paint and stain until you end up with the perfect patina for your project.

the bottom board has been sanded and the one above it has had another layer of stain added after sanding to cover up any "new wood" look

other embellishment ideas

wheels/casters

Putting a side table or small cart on wheels is a fun way to give a piece additional personality and versatility.

numbers and letters and symbols, oh my

Adding your favorite quotes or numbers is an easy way to customize anything.

▸ You can see how we used foam letters to create a stencil when we made the Headboard in Chapter 6.
▸ We used a great old set of brass stencils (that I got from my mom—thanks, Mom!) to make the Eclectic Directional Sign in Chapter 5 and to add a name plaque to the Large Dog Bed in Chapter 6.

you don't even need to cut out the letters you print on the home printer; trace them with enough force to leave an indentation on your wood to indicate where to paint

- I also like just printing out block-style letters on our home printer and cutting them out, tracing around them, and painting inside the lines.
- If the letters you print out are too small or intricate to cut out, you can trace over them using some force so you create a small indentation in your wood, and then paint the lettering from there like I did with this word art made from pallet slats.
- I've used a simple image-transfer technique that requires only a home printer and some white glue to make a few unique projects. The tutorial for making this project can be found at *http://thespacebetweenblog.net/2013/06/10/you-are-the*.

use only your home printer with some white glue and water to create this image-transfer technique that works great on wood

this accent wall in our guest bedroom was made using reclaimed 1×6s and alternating one row of wood with one row of ¾" rope. find the full tutorial at *http://thespacebetweenblog.net/2014/05/12/rope-and-wood-accent-wall-reclaimed-wood/*

rope

In addition to the rope around the Rustic Wood Clock in Chapter 2 and for the Hanging Bed in Chapter 5, rope can add a bit of a nautical flair to any of the projects in this book. Wrap some rope around table legs or put a row of rope in between your pallet slats, or maybe even add some rope handles.

To prevent your rope from fraying, dip the end tied with painter's tape in white glue and let it dry overnight. The glue will dry clear and hold your rope together after you remove the tape.

cutouts

Any of the wall art or furniture pieces can be customized using shapes or cutouts. Cut the pallet slats into a diamond or even circle shape, or give one edge some flare with a wavy cut.

potato stamping

Like the stars we made for the American Flag in Chapter 4, a potato stamp is an easy way to add an image to anything you make.

Just cut your shape out of a potato and apply a thin layer of paint. Use a paper towel to wipe up any accumulation of paint around the edges to prevent clumping.

the end

Here we are, 35 tutorials, a bunch of tips and tricks, and a handful of embellishment ideas later. Ideas for you to take these projects and create beautiful, functional pieces for your own home. Here is where I hand you the ~~nail gun~~ reins and you tackle your next great creation. It feels like the last day of summer and we're standing on the diving board hand in hand and about to dive into the deep end of the pool for the very first time, all by ourselves. But I'm confident you could even do a back flip if you really wanted to. Take these projects and build off them (no pun intended, seriously!). Make them bigger and better and badder—badder in a gooder way, of course. And stop in every once in a while to say hi. You can find all kinds of behind-the-scenes book stuff at *http://thespacebetweenblog.net/book*. We're talking outtakes, what was *really* going on behind the camera, blogs, and websites that inspire me and one big ol' project fail that definitely did not make it into the book. Oh yeah, and there's that pesky house remodel we're tackling in between.

So here, take it—the nail gun, that is—and create something you adore out of something that didn't cost you a thing. And make the most of it, your little (or maybe big) space between.

index

about the author

Karah is the owner, blogger, and DIYer behind the blog *the space between*, where she chronicles her adventures to make the most of her every space. Although she finds herself moving every few years as her husband pursues his career, she is passionate about creating a home to love through upcycling, repurposing, and some hardcore home renovations. She's currently knee-deep in a full DIY renovation of their 1950s conch-style house in Key West, Florida. Picture drywall dust everywhere, paint in her hair, and pallets collecting in the yard just waiting to be turned into a piece of furniture or eclectic storage solution.

In addition to the blog, Karah can be found online here:

▸ Pinterest: *www.pinterest.com/ kbunde*
▸ Facebook: *www.facebook.com/ TheSpaceBetweenBlog1*
▸ Twitter: *www.twitter.com/ karahs_space*
▸ Instagram: *www.instagram.com/ thespacebetweenblog*
▸ Google+: *http://plus.google .com/u/0/+KarahBunde*

Cheers to making the most of *the space between* . . . you know the one, that little space between where you've been and where you're going.